Men-at-Arms • 485

Polish Armies of the Partitions 1770–1794

Vincent W. Rospond • Illustrated by Raffaele Ruggeri

Series editor Martin Windrow

First published in Great Britain in 2013 by Osprey Publishing, Midland House, West Way, Botley, Oxford, OX2 0PH, UK 43-01 21st Street, Suite 220B, Long Island City, NY 11101, USA E-mail: info@ospreypublishing.com
OSPREY PUBLISHING IS PART OF THE OSPREY GROUP

A CIP catalogue record for this book is available from the British Library

Print ISBN: 978 1 84908855 8
PDF ebook ISBN: 978 1 84908856 5
ePub ebook ISBN: 978 1 78200 911 5

Editor: Martin Windrow
Index by Rob Munro
Typeset in Helvetica Neue and ITC New Baskerville
Map by JB Illustrations
Originated by PDQ Media, Bungay, UK
Printed in China through Worldprint Ltd

13 14 15 16 17 18 10 9 8 7 6 5 4 3 2 1

Osprey Publishing is supporting the Woodland Trust, the UK's leading woodland conservation charity, by funding the dedication of trees.

www.ospreypublishing.com

Dedication

This book is dedicated to my parents, who always worried about my fascination with history, but encouraged me anyway; to my wife, for her patience with my obsessions; and to Florentyna Kostka, who told me stories.

Author's note

One of the challenges of researching the Polish-Lithuanian army of the late 18th century is that the objective of the partitioning powers was to erase the name of Poland from history as if it had never existed. Time, and two World Wars, have aided their destructive work, but the dedication of historians and individual researchers all over the world has brought to light more information for our study (though unavoidably complicated by the differing spellings of proper names in sources using four different languages). The information presented here aims to give – within the inevitable limitations of space – a general outline of the army and its organization during the last 34 years of the Commonwealth. This period saw the activity of two generals who influenced the American Revolution (Pulaski and Kosciuszko); the creation of the first true written constitution in European history; and the development of tactics of which the effects would be felt well into the 19th century.

Acknowledgements

The folks at Arsenal.pl were extremely supportive; they pointed me towards some very useful resources – especially Andrzej Kropek. Special thanks to Dariusz Wyrozebski for his comments and notes; and to Raffaele Ruggeri for all his hard work on the plates. Unless specifically credited otherwise, all illustrations are free-of-copyright images from the author's collection. 'NAMW' indicates the National Army Museum, Warsaw.

Artist's Note

Readers may care to note that the original paintings from which the colour plates in this book were prepared are available for private sale. All reproduction copyright whatsoever is retained by the Publishers. All enquiries should be addressed to:
Raffaele Ruggeri, Via Indipendenza 22, Bologna, 40121, Italy
The Publishers regret that they can enter into no correspondence upon this matter.

OPPOSITE
Tadeusz Kosciuszko (1746–1817), leader of the national uprising against Russia and Prussia in 1794, was often painted wearing the *sukmana* coat of the Krakow peasants who helped his troops fight the Russians – see Plate H1. A minor nobleman from the Grand Duchy, he enrolled in 1765 in the King's Corps of Cadets, which gave poor but promising young men a broad military and civil education for national service. After extensive further studies in Paris, he offered his sword to the American Congress in 1776. He became chief engineer of Washington's Continental Army, and a friend of Thomas Jefferson, whose work on the Declaration of Independence inspired his hopes for his homeland. Returning to Poland in 1784, he distinguished himself in command of the 3rd Crown Division during the 1792 war in defence of the new liberal constitution, and was one of the first recipients of the *Virtuti Militari* cross. As commander-in-chief (*naczelnik*) during the 1794 insurrection, he was wounded and captured at the battle of Maciejowice. Released in 1796, he died in exile in Switzerland, but his remains were later returned to Poland to lie in a crypt in Wawel Cathedral, Krakow. (Portrait by Kazimierz Wojniakowski, *c.*1810)

POLISH ARMIES OF THE PARTITIONS 1770–1794

HISTORICAL BACKGROUND

By the 18th century the unified Kingdom of Poland and Grand Duchy of Lithuania (collectively known at this period as 'the Commonwealth', but in this text, for simplicity, often called simply 'Poland') had been a major power in East-Central Europe for more than 300 years. Poland, including what became East Prussia, Pomerania and part of Southern Ukraine, was referred to as 'the Crown', and Lithuania, incorporating much of Belarus and Northern Ukraine, as 'the Duchy'.

During that century, however, the Commonwealth suffered from chronic internal weaknesses. Historically, Poland did not have a hereditary but rather an elective monarchy, chosen by factions among the quarrelsome aristocracy. While the majority of the peasants still lived in serfdom, this *szlachta* class, jealous of their privileges, used their powers in the *Sejm* (parliament) to prevent effective central government or social reform. This squabbling reduced the Commonwealth to the status of a client of neighbouring Russia, and Moscow exercised decisive influence over the Sejm. As the century progressed, rivalries between Russia, the Habsburg Austro-Hungarian Empire and the increasingly vigorous Prussia would see all three powers manipulating Polish politics for their own ends.

During this period of political and military decline, from the end of the Great Northern War (1717) until the First Partition (1772), the Poles fought only each other. Under a Saxon king, Frederick Augustus, in 1718 Poland was reduced to a Russian protectorate, its armies limited to 18,000 Crown and 6,000 Duchy troops. Russia's status as guarantor of Polish security allowed it a free hand in the country's internal affairs, and when the king died in 1733 a Russian army marched in to compel the election of his son. Prussia also became a partner in this Russian policy, and used Poland as a source of men, materials and resources.

On the death in 1764 of King August III, the Russian Tsarina Catherine II the Great applied pressure on the Sejm to elect her former lover Stanislaw Poniatowski as king in place of August's son. Poniatowski was a son of a noble Polish clan, but not a 'power player' in Polish politics. However, as the new King Stanislaw II August he soon showed himself unhappy in his intended role as simply a catspaw for Russia. A child of the Enlightenment, he dreamed of restoring his country's fortunes, and he promoted modernizing

Stanislaw August Poniatowski, the last King of Poland (r.1764–94), who reigned as Stanislaw II August. Catherine the Great of Russia engineered his election to the Polish throne, and he was often vilified as a tool of the Russians. However, his position was impossibly difficult, and he has more recently been given credit for his efforts on behalf of his country. He created industries, was a patron of the arts and sciences, and helped to write the liberal Constitution of 3 May 1791, which drew upon both American and British ideas. (From a portrait by Giovanni Battista Lampri, 1788)

reforms – including some that would give the monarchy a stronger hand over the nobility. This threatened the interests of Russia, which depended upon a fractious and disunited Polish aristocracy to keep the monarchy weak and manipulable.

In 1767–68 the Russian ambassador Repnin forced the Sejm to pass measures favouring followers of the Orthodox Church. Although this treaty also guaranteed the privileges ('Golden Liberties') of the nobility, its demonstration of the Russian-installed king's impotence enraged a powerful group of Catholic traditionalist noblemen. They accordingly formed a Confederation at the town of Bar, and declared war against Russia. This initiated a civil war that led, a few years later, to the First Partition of Poland.

Shocked by this disaster, far-sighted Poles worked patiently to prepare the ground for reforms. These culminated in the work of the 'Great Sejm' (1788–92), which proclaimed the bold new liberal constitution of 3 May 1791. Another group of conservative aristocrats, provoked by this threat to their privileges, then formed the Targowica Confederation and actually invited Russian military intervention (a treachery that would see several of them hanged during the 1794 insurrection).

After the War in Defence of the Constitution in 1792 ended in defeat and a Second Partition, orders to disband Polish forces provided the immediate spark for Kosciuszko's Insurrection in spring 1794. Its heroic failure doomed the Polish nation to the Third Partition, and complete political extinction at the hands of Russia, Prussia and Austria.

CHRONOLOGY

1764   Stanislaw Poniatowski elected as King Stanislaw II August, on Russian insistence.

1765   King's Corps of Cadets founded, to prepare promising young men for service.

1767   Army strength reduced to 12,000 men, on Russian insistence.

1768   Cardinal Laws passed, granting – among other provisions – emancipation of Orthodox dissenters, and are enforced by Russian troops. Bar Confederation formed (**29 February**) by leaders including Kazimierz Pulaski, Karol Radziwill and Joachim Potocki. Encouraged by French diplomats, the Confederation declares war on Russia. King Stanislaw's mediation efforts fail, and he sends royal forces under Grand Hetman Franciszek Branicki against Confederates in Ukraine (**April–June**). Peasant and Cossack uprisings against the monarchy in Ukraine (**May 1768–June 1769**) take some pressure off Confederates, but royal forces secure Krakow (**22 August**). Outbreak of Russo-Turkish War of 1768–74 (**September**) draws some Russian troops away. Fighting in Belarus (**August–October**); Confederates surrender at Nesvizh (**26 October**).

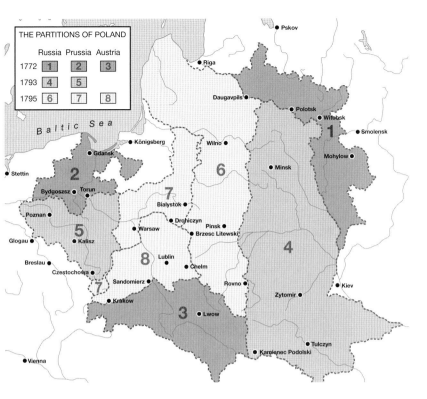

THE PARTITIONS OF POLAND

	Russia	Prussia	Austria
1772	1	2	3
1793	4	5	
1795	6	7	8

Sketch map of Polish and Lithuanian territory appropriated by Russia, Prussia and Austria during the three partitions. Poland had been the third largest country in Europe, but during the Bar Confederation civil war (1768–72) both Austria and Prussia annexed border regions. The First Partition cost Poland about one-third of its territory and one-half of its population; in August 1772 foreign troops moved in to secure the annexed territories, although guerrilla resistance continued for years. In the Second Partition of 1793, following Poland's defeat in the War in Defence of the Constitution, Russia and Prussia took most of Lithuania's remaining territory in what is now Belarus and western Ukraine, and Prussia the remainder of what became East Prussia and Pomerania; this left Poland with a population of only some 4 million, and a ruined economy.

A preliminary third agreement between Russia, Prussia and Austria in October 1794 pre-dated the crushing of the Kosciuszko Insurrection by a month. Under final terms agreed in January 1797 the three powers divided up the whole remaining national territory, and Poland disappeared from the map of Europe for 123 years. (Map by JB Illustrations)

1769   Confederates set up 'Generality' at Biala near Austrian border, and receive French advisors. After early successes in Lithuania, they are defeated at Bialystok (**16 July**) and Orzechowo (**13 September**).

1770   Confederates suffer defeats at Dobre (**20 January**) and Blonie (**12 February**), but French Gen Dumouriez improves their organization. Confederation Council declares King Stanislaw dethroned (**22 October**).

1771   Russian Gen Suvorov defeats Confederates at Lanckorona (**21 May**), and they suffer a further defeat at Stolowicze (**23 September**). Confederate attempt to kidnap King Stanislaw fails (**3 November**), and costs Confederation foreign support.

1772   Russia, Prussia and Austria agree first partition of Poland (**February**), which the king is powerless to resist. Final Confederate defeats; fall of Wawel Castle, Krakow (**28 April**), and surrender of Jasna Gora monastery (**13 August**) and Pulaski's garrison in Czestochowa (**18 August**) effectively end the war, although rebels in Zagorz monastery hold out until 28 November.

1773   Sejm ratifies treaty of partition (**30 September**). Some 5,000 Poles are deported to Siberia.

1775   Permanent Council abolishes private armies of the nobility.
1776   Cavalry organized into National Cavalry brigades.
1782   Purchase of army ranks abolished.
1788   The 'Great Sejm' (1788–92) institutes major military reforms, and authorizes a 100,000-strong army. Russia rejects Polish offer of military assistance against the Ottomans.

1789	King Stanislaw authorizes appointment as major-generals of Prince Ludwig of Wurttemberg, Jozef Poniatowski and Tadeusz Kosciuszko.
1790	Treaty of alliance with Prussia.
1791	Proclamation by Sejm, with king's encouragement, of liberal Constitution (**3 May**). Welcomed by progressives, and at first tolerated by Prussia and Austria, this is resisted by conservative magnates, including Stanislaw Potocki, Franciszek Branicki, Szymon Kossakowski, Bishop Josef Kossakowski and Ignacy Massalski.
1792	The conservative Targowica Confederation – whose articles are actually drafted by the Russian Gen Popov, and signed in St Petersburg – requests Russian intervention (**14 May**). War in Defence of the Constitution: Russian troops cross border (**15 May**), and Ludwig of Wurttemberg fails to resist their advance in Lithuania. Prussia abandons alliance and invades to further its own interests. Under Jozef Poniatowski and Kosciuszko, small but well-led Commonwealth forces conduct a skilful fighting retreat from Ukraine, buying time at Zielenice (**18 June**), Markuszow (**16 July**), Wlodzimierz (**17 July**), and Dubienka (**18 July**); but King Stanislaw gives way to Confederates' demands, and orders ceasefire (**24 July**).
1793	Russia and Prussia agree terms of second partition (**23 January**), ratified by the Sejm under duress that summer. Half of army ordered to disband, and most of remainder to be transferred into Russian and Prussian armies. Russian troops arrest patriot leaders.
1794	Gen Madalinski refuses order to disband his 1st National Cavalry Bde, and marches on Krakow (**12 March**). General Tadeusz Kosciuszko proclaims general insurrection under his chief command (**24 March**). Battle of Raclawice: with 4,000 troops and 2,000 peasant militia, Kosciuszko defeats Russian Gen Denisov's 5,000 men (**4 April**). Jan Kilinski leads uprising in Warsaw, forcing withdrawal of Russian garrison in bloody street-fighting (**17–19 April**). Kosciuszko issues Polaniec Proclamation, freeing the serfs and granting them civil rights (**7 May**). Prussian troops enter northern Poland to co-operate with Russians (**10 May**). Kosciuszko defeated at Szczekociny by Russo-Prussian army (**6 June**), and falls back to fortify Warsaw. Patriot Gen Jozef Zajaczek defeated at Chelm (**8 June**). Prussians occupy Krakow (**15 June**). 100,000 Russian and Prussian troops arrive before Warsaw (**22 July**). Patriots surrender to Russians at Wilno, Lithuania (**12 August**). Patriot manoeuvres in north-west force Prussians to withdraw from siege of Warsaw (**20 August**). Kosciuszko's 35,000-strong garrison repulses Russian assaults (**26 August–5 September**), and Russians lift siege. Russian Gen Suvorov marches to join Gen Fersen before Warsaw, winning actions at Krupczyce (**17 September**) and Terespol (**19 September**). In Pomerania, patriot Gen Dabrowski captures Bydgoszcz from Prussians

(**2 October**). Kosciuszko marches out to prevent link-up of Fersen's and Suvorov's armies, but his own second division is delayed, and he is caught between them. Battle of Maciejowice: Kosciuszko defeated and captured by Russians (**10 October**). Treaty agreeing partition of Poland signed by Russia, Prussia and Austria (**24 October**). Battle of Praga (**2–4 November**): 24,000 Russian troops break into Warsaw suburb defended by patriots under Tomasz Wawrzecki amid great destruction and bloodshed, and Warsaw falls (**5 November**). Wawrzecki withdraws south, and surrenders last troops (**16 November**). Purges and massive deportations of Polish patriots follow Russian occupation.

1797 Final settlement of tripartite Third Partition agreed (**16 January**).

THE ARMIES OF 1764–72

Organization of the Commonweath armies

The Crown and Duchy armies operated independently of one another, but were organized as mirror images; in some respects regular troops followed a Saxon model, inherited from the Saxon monarchy of 1697–1764.

In theory the overall commander of the Commonwealth forces was a Grand Hetman, appointed by the king. Under him, a Field Hetman exercised operational control of each army. Divisions and brigades were not established, but were organized as the situation dictated under the command of major-generals. The king nominally controlled the Guard, comprising a regiment of infantry and one of cavalry in both the Crown and the Duchy. The artillery was under the command of its own general; batteries were dispersed throughout the Commonwealth in fortresses, and integrated within infantry regiments.

In 1765 infantry regiments were organized in two battalions, each having one grenadier and five musketeer companies. In addition, each regiment had an artillery company with four guns. Separate grenadier and fusilier regiments had two battalions each of six companies. The aristocratic proprietor of the regiment was the *Szef* ('Chief'), by whose name the regiment was known, although numbering in the Line was beginning during this period. Everyday operational command was exercised by the colonel. Throughout this period battalions and companies were habitually understrength, and prior to 1772 regular units often had many officers and enlisted ranks absent on leave at any given time. The government was therefore forced to rely upon the 'private armies' of local magnates to help maintain order, and a number of these were later enrolled into the regular Line.

A romantic reconstructed portrait of Kazimierz Pulaski, painted by Arthur Szyk in the 1940s. Pulaski was a charismatic leader of the Bar Confederation forces, whose fight for their religion and ancient rights against Russia actually hindered attempts to reform Poland's archaic institutions, and precipitated the First Partition. The Confederate Council, based initially in Silesia and later in Austrian territory, at first benefited from foreign (particularly French) encouragement. This faded with time, and the attempt by Pulaski and others to kidnap the king in November 1771 provoked Austria to expel the Confederates. Pulaski eventually fled to North America, where he led the Continental Army's cavalry until his death at Savannah in 1779. (1940, author's collection)

Portrait by an unknown artist of Gen Jan Henryk Dabrowski as a division commander; in 1794 he led a breakout by troops from Warsaw, and wreaked havoc on the Prussian border. After the crushing of the Insurrection he tried to serve his nation by setting up the Polish Legions in Italy. His coat seems to be a double-breasted *litewka* in midnight blue, faced and lined with crimson at the collar, cuffs and partly opened breast. Collar and cuffs bear two lines of silver lace in the Polish generals' traditional 'folded ribbon' design, and the thickly fringed epaulettes are silver. The pouch belt is buff, with silver picker chains passing from a Polish eagle down to a trophy of arms. Note the ornate decoration of the sword hilt, in silver and black niello. (NAMW; author's collection)

1770: Crown cavalry

Chief	Designation	Kontusz	Facings	Zupan	Hat	Pennant
Poniatowski	Guard Dragoons	Buff	Red	-	Black	
	Pancerni	Blue	Red	Red	Red	Blue/red
	Hussars	Red	Blue	Blue	Blue	Red/blue
Wojno	King's Lancers	Green	Crimson	-	Crimson	Red/green
Raczynski	Podstoli Horse	Cornflower blue	Yellow	Yellow	Light Blue	Blue/yellow

1770: Crown dragoons

Chief	Designation	Coat	Facings	Buttons	Lace	Notes
Kozlowski	Queen's	Green	Red	Silver	White	
Czapski	Prince's	Red	Green	Silver	White	
Raczynski		Green	Red	Silver	White	
Sulkowski		Green	Red	Silver	White	
Branicki	Grand Hetman's	Green	Black	Silver	White	
Rzewuski	Field Hetman's	Green	Red	Silver	White	

1770: Grand Duchy of Lithuania cavalry

Chief	Designation	Katanka	Facings	Zupan	Hat	Pennant
Grabowski	Horse Guards	Red	Blue	-	Black	-
	Petyhorcy	Blue	Red	White	Blue	Blue/red
Sapieha	Grand Hetman Light Horse	Green	Red	-	Red	Green/red
Bielak	Potocki Tartars	Red	Yellow	-	Black	-
Poniatowski		White	Green	Green	Green	Red/green

1770: Grand Duchy of Lithuania dragoons

Chief	Designation	Coat	Facings	Buttons	Lace	Notes
Oginski	Duke's	Green	Red	Gold	White	(1775) 5th GD Inf
Oginski	Grand Hetman's	Green	Black	Gold	White	(1775) 2nd GD Inf
Sapieha	Field Hetman's	Green	Red	Gold	White	(1775) 4th GD Inf

The Commonwealth's armies had evolved from small organic groups. Independent cavalry units were called *chorągwi* (loosely, companies), of which several might be combined into a *pułk* (regiment). In the regular forces the cavalry company/squadron was termed a 'banner'. In the Crown lands, cavalry consisted of 16 banners of hussars (which in the Polish context meant heavy cavalry, formerly armoured); 76 banners of *pancerni* (medium cavalry); 14 banners of light cavalry, and 7 regiments of dragoons. The Grand Duchy's cavalry were 6 banners of hussars, 25 banners of medium cavalry (*petyhorcy*), 12 banners of Tartars, 8 banners of Cossacks, and 4 regiments of dragoons.

Impression of the wounding and capture of Kosciuszko at the battle of Maciejowice. This effectively brought the 1794 Insurrection to a close, since no other single person could unite the different factions within the insurgent government or army. (Artist unknown; author's collection)

Uniform of an officer of grenadiers of the Crown Foot Guards, 1750s; this Saxon style of uniform was still in use in the 1770s (compare with Plates C2 & C3). The mitre cap has a gilt, cut-out brass plate backed with red cloth. The red coat is faced with medium or sky blue (now much faded); both it and the blue waistcoat have gold buttons and lace. Note the large gorget, and the large decorative pocket flaps on the waistcoat. (NAMW, author's collection)

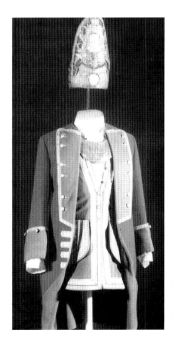

Uniforms

For the infantry, the uniform was the long-tailed coat of Western European style. This was red for Crown troops and blue for Duchy troops, with collar, cuffs, lapels and turnbacks in contrasting facing/lining colours to differentiate the regiments. The cuffs and lapels were approximately 5cm (1.96in) wide and the collar about 5cm high. The waistcoat was white or buff, with coloured trim along the edges and pockets. Soldiers wore red or black stocks (cravats). Knee-breeches were white, with black thigh-length cloth gaiters. Headgear were black tricorne hats with white trim for musketeers, and brass-plated bearskin or mitre caps for grenadiers and fusiliers.

In addition, the King's Guard and the Hetman regiments had elite Janissary and Hungarian companies, independent of the regimental structure. The Janissaries wore a Turkish-inspired costume: a cylindrical felt *börk* hat, extending into a sleeve that hung down the back. By the late 18th century what had originally been a brass headband with a central plume-holder had moved upwards in a sort of stylized 'mitre plate', still with a plume-holder. They also wore baggy trousers and a long *kaftan* coat, with the front corners tucked up into the belt to free the legs. Hungarian companies wore that country's traditional tight breeches, some with embroidered 'knots' on the thighs.

In the cavalry, hussar companies wore a low, four-cornered cap that came to be known as the *konfederatka*; this had a crown rising from a bottom band of fleece or fur, and sported white feathers. The upper garment was a crimson *kontusz* with blue facings (a thigh-length coat, usually with the sleeves split for wearing thrown back behind the shoulders). This was worn over a long blue *zupan* (a long-sleeved robe, buttoned at the front, originally ankle-length but now sometimes seen shortened to the knee). Weapons were a lance, sabre and firearms, and some still wore breastplates. Traditionally, hussar units had been made up of two classes of troops: the *towarzycz* ('comrade' – the elite who rode in the front rank), and the *pocztowy* ('retainer', who rode in the rear rank). During the period of the Partitions the Line cavalry retained this structure, with differentiating uniform features. 'Comrades' typically carried lances, while 'retainers' more often did not.

1770: Crown infantry and technical corps

Chief	No.	Designation	Collar & cuffs	Lapels	Buttons	Grenadiers
Czartoryski		Guards	Blue	Blue	Gold	Bearskin
Golcz	1	Queen Jadwiga	Black	Black	Silver	Bearskin
Witten	2	Crown Prince	White	White	Gold	Bearskin
Branicki	3	Grand Hetman	Green	Green	Gold	Brass mitre
Branicki	4	Field Hetman	Light blue	Light blue	Silver	Bearskin
Potocki	5	Fusiliers	Black	Black	Gold	n/a
Sulkowski	6	Lanowy	Green	Green	Silver	Bearskin
Brühl		Artillery	Black	Black	Silver	n/a

1770: Crown infantry independent companies

Unit	Jacket	Trim	Facings	Trousers	Hat
Grand Hetman Janissary	Red	White	Green	Red	White
Grand Hetman Hungarian	Light blue	Yellow	Red	Light blue	Black
Field Hetman Hungarian	Light blue	Yellow	Green	Light blue	Black
Grand Marshal Hungarian	Blue	Silver	Orange	White	Brass-peaked
Warsaw Militia	Light blue	Yellow	Light blue	Light blue	Black

1770: Grand Duchy of Lithuania infantry and technical corps

Chief	No.	Designation	Collar & cuffs	Lapels	Buttons	Grenadiers
Czartoryski		Guard	Blue	Blue	Silver	Bearskin
Oginski	1	Grand Hetman	White	White	Gold	Mitre
Sosnowski	2	Field Hetman	Black	Black	Gold	-
Massalski		Artillery	Black	Black	Gold	Black
Cronenmann		Freikorps Artillery	Red	Red	Gold	Brass mitre

1770: Grand Duchy of Lithuania infantry independent companies

Unit	Jacket	Trim	Facings	Trousers	Hat
Grand Hetman Janissary	Red	Black	Black	Red	Red
Field Hetman Janissary	Red	Green	Green	Red	Green
Grand Hetman Hungarian	Light blue	Yellow	Yellow	Light blue	Black
Field Hetman Hungarian	Light blue	Yellow	Light blue	Black	
Freikompanie Art Grenadier	Green	Red	Red	White	Mitre

The *pancerni* medium cavalry companies (in the Grand Duchy, *petyhorcy*) wore these same uniform colours in reverse – a blue *kontusz* over a red *zupan*. Light cavalry wore a felt or wool *kuczma* Cossack-style cap; a 'stocking' shape about 15.25–20cm (6–8in) high, this had a fleece or fur bottom band that could be rolled down over the ears in cold weather. A *katanka* (a short-sleeved decorative jacket) was worn over a long *zupan* in a contrasting colour. These troops also carried a sabre, a musket, and a light lance about 1.8–2.4m (6–8ft) long, surmounted by a swallow-tailed pennant horizontally halved in the two regimental uniform colours. Dragoons wore short infantry coats in green with regimental facing colours on the collars, lapels and cuffs; boots were worn for mounted duty and gaiters for dismounted. They were armed with a sword, pistols and a musketoon.

Artillerymen of both nations wore green jackets with black facings. The gun carriages and other equipment were painted red – the traditional Saxon colour, held over from the former monarchy – with black metal fittings. For most of the Bar Confederation War artillery pieces were leftovers at least 50 years old.

All officers wore a sash in mixed red and silver, with fringed ends tied on the right side. Company officers wore their shoulder straps (epaulettes) on the left shoulder, regimental senior staff and general officers on both shoulders. Non-commissioned officers were distinguished by lace around the collar, cuffs and shoulder straps, and trumpeters by lace on the collars, cuffs and shoulders.

The Bar Confederation, 1768–72

This had no central organization; the rebels were a miscellany of small local groups, widely dispersed and each with its own organization and goals. Because most participants had some military experience they were generally organized in companies each under a captain, modelled on the Crown or Duchy forces with which they were familiar. They lacked a co-ordinated strategy, but initially mounted hit-and-run cavalry attacks backed up by some infantry. As foreign advisors arrived to assist their cause they began to abandon free-ranging mobile warfare in favour of capturing towns to act as bases. Making proper use of artillery required the advice of technical experts, and garrisoning towns demanded greater numbers of infantry.

There was some attempt to uniform the cavalry in the traditional *kontusz* and *zupan* with an elongated *konfederatka*, but in practice their dress quickly degenerated into anything that was available (see Plate A). Infantry were often dressed in everyday peasant clothing, sometimes sporting the family distinctions of the noblemen who raised them. Eventually, as support arrived first from Prussia and later from Austria, some Confederate infantry were uniformed in the Western manner, including white military coats.

A major-general of the Commonwealth, 1780s, shown in a blue coat faced and lined with red, over white smallclothes laced with gold. This costume style would have been indistinguishable from that of any other European army of the period; the collar lace was even copied from the Prussian army. (Gabriel Raspe, 1783; NAMW courtesy of Arsenal.org.pl)

THE ARMY OF 1772–91

During the Bar Confederation civil war of 1768–72, Antoni Madalinski (1739–1805) was a supporter of the Confederates. As a general in 1794, it was he who set the Kosciuszko Insurrection in motion when he refused to disband his 1st National Cavalry Brigade. His march on Krakow forced Kosciuszko to initiate the rebellion that today bears his name. (Artist unknown; author's collection)

Organization

It was around this time that the first army manuals were developed, and a stress began to be placed upon national obligations. The organizational structure remained largely unchanged, but during the 1770s the Crown army was formed into four administrative divisions by province ('voivodeship', *wojewodztwo*):

1776: Crown cavalry						
Chief	Designation	Kontusz	Facings	Zupan	Hat	Pennant
Poniatowski	Guard Dragoons	Buff	Red	-	Black	(red tabard garment)
Luba	1st Wielkopolski	Blue	Red	Red	Red	Blue/red
Dzierzek	1st Ukrainian	Blue	Red	White	Red	Red with white Maltese cross
Zielonka	2nd Ukrainian	Light blue	Crimson	White	Light blue	Red with white Maltese cross
Lubowidzki	3rd Ukrainian	Blue	Red	Red	Blue	Blue/red
Wojno	King's Lancers	Green	Red	-	Red	Green/red
Anastaszy	Adv Guard	Dark blue	Red	Red	Red	Blue/red
Kajetan	Adv Guard	Green	Black	Red	Green	Green/black

1776: Crown dragoons						
Chief	Designation	Coat	Facings	Buttons	Lace	Notes (1789>)
Kozlowski	Queen's	Green	Red	Silver	White	1st Adv Gd
Branicki	Grand Hetman's	Green	Black	Silver	White	2nd Adv Gd
Rzewuski	Field Hetman's	Green	Red	Silver	White	3rd Adv Gd
Raczynski		Green	Red	Silver	White	9th Inf
Czapski	Prince's	Red	Blue	Silver	White	8th Inf
Potocki		Green	Cornflower blue	Silver	White	7th Inf

1776: Grand Duchy of Lithuania cavalry						
Chief	Designation	Jacket	Facings	Zupan	Hat	Pennant
Grabowski	Duke's Horse Guards	Red	Blue	-	Black	-
Tykiewicz	Hussars of Kowienska	Dark blue	Red	White	Red	Blue/red
Chominski	Petyhorsk	Dark blue	Yellow	White	Black	Blue/yellow
Baranowski	1st Adv Guard	White	Yellow	Yellow	Yellow	Yellow/light blue
Jelenski	2nd Adv Guard	White	Orange	Orange	Orange	Blue/yellow
Romanowski	3rd Adv Guard	White	Blue	Blue	Blue	Blue/yellow
Bielak	4th Adv Guard	White	Red	Red	Red	Red/yellow
Hallaszewski	5th Adv Guard	White	Green	Green	Green	Yellow/blue
Azulewicz	Tartars	Red	Yellow	-	Yellow	Red/yellow

Wielkopolska or Greater Poland (west and central, the main
cities being Poznan and Kalisz).

Malopolska or Lesser Poland (southern, with centres at
Krakow, Lublin and Lwow).

Wolyn (Volhynia, historically straddling the Ukrainian border;
this lay between the eastern central area of Masovia, centred
on Warsaw, and the Bug river to its south-east).

Podlaskie (north-east, centred on Drohiczyn).

Lithuania formed the single administrative district of Wilno
(modern Vilnius).

By 1776 the Line cavalry was organized into National Cavalry
brigades. In 1784 a brigade consisted of 24 companies/squadrons
of 144 troopers, while the Guard Cavalry had eight troops of
47 men. The cavalryman was equipped with a pair of pistols,
a sword, a lance or a short musket – dragoons also had a bayonet.

Both armies had artillery, engineers and pontoneers grouped
in a separate administrative element known as 'equipment'
(in our accompanying tables, 'technical corps'). During this
period an artillery train was organized under army rather than
civilian control. The artillery was gradually re-equipped with
cannon at first based on Austrian designs, but by 1779 it was
beginning to follow French models. The Crown began to cast artillery
for the first time in 80 years, and by the end of 1789 the foundries had
produced 185 guns in various calibres, in addition to 58 privately-cast
regimental guns. The standard calibres were 3-, 6-, 8-, 12- and 18-pounders;
there were also 6in and 8in howitzers, and a variety of mortars.

Uniforms

An ordinance of 9 February 1776 simplified the cavalry uniforms,
transforming both hussars and *pancerni* into 'lancers' within the new
National Cavalry brigades. The former hussar 'banners' wore a crimson
cap and *kontusz* with dark blue collar, cuffs and turnbacks. Crown troops
had white-metal buttons and Duchy troops brass. The *pancerni* 'banners'
had a dark blue cap and *kontusz* with crimson collar, cuffs and turnbacks,
with buttons as above. Under the *kontusz* they wore a long white *zupan*.
A drawing of National Cavalry uniforms based on the 1776 ordinances
shows the lance pennant for Crown troops as crimson with a white
Maltese cross centred towards the shaft, and Duchy brigades with
pennants halved in blue over the facing colour.

An ordinance of 9 February 1778 changed the uniform style again.
The National Cavalry *towarzycz* had a *konfederatka* with a crimson crown,
a white band above the black lambswool bottom edging-band, and a
white plume. The jacket was a dark blue *kontusz* with crimson facings,
over a white waistcoat; some officers still wore a white *zupan*. The trousers
were crimson with a blue sidestripe extending into a band around
the bottom. Troopers wore crimson belts. The shoulder cords, epaulettes
and belt plates were silver. To differentiate the classes, the *potczowy*
trooper wore both jacket and trousers in blue, with collar, cuffs, facings,
trouser sidestripe and bottom band in crimson. Their cap was either
a black mirliton-style *giwer*, a quilted cap or a fur *kolpak* busby. The latter
might have a red top or 'bag'; cords were silver and crimson, and
the plume white.

Towarzycz and *pocztowy*, 1st
Advance Guard Regt of the
Crown, 1780s. They differ in
their headgear and details of
their uniforms. Both wear
crimson caps; a dark blue
katanka over-jacket trimmed
and faced crimson, over a white
long-sleeved waistcoat (*zupanik*)
with pointed crimson cuffs; and
dark blue riding trousers with
scalloped crimson stripes and
pale leather reinforcements.
The 'comrade' has more jacket
trim; what seem to be flat
white epaulettes instead of
redshoulder straps; yellow
half-boots instead of black,
and sword slings instead of a
white frog. His lance pennant
is blue over crimson. This
transitional style of uniform
was typical for Advance Guard
and other light cavalry
between the 1760s and 1789.
(Gabriel Raspe, NAMW;
author's collection)

A print of 1781 showing an officer and musketeer of the 2nd Crown Foot Regt 'Crown Prince' (in 1776, Witten's; in 1792, Wodzicki's). The Saxon-style scarlet uniform – in this case faced with white, and with silver 'metal' – lasted from 1772 to 1789. (Gabriel Raspe, NAMW; author's collection)

1776: Crown infantry and technical corps

Chief	No.	Designation	Collar & cuffs	Lapels	Buttons	Grenadiers
Czartoryski		Guards	Blue	Blue	Gold	Bearskin
Golcz	1	Queen Jadwiga	Black	Black	Silver	Bearskin
Witten	2	Crown Prince	White	White	Silver	Bearskin
Branicki	3	Grand Hetman	Green	Green	Gold	Brass mitre
Branicki	4	Field Hetman	Light blue	Light blue	Silver	Bearskin
Potocki	5	Fusiliers	Black	Black	Silver	N/A
Sulkowski	6	Lanowy	Green	Green	Silver	Bearskin
Raczynski	7		Cornflower blue	Cornflower blue	Silver	
Rydzynski	8		Yellow	Yellow	Silver	Brass mitre
Lubormirski	9	Grenadiers	Blue	Blue	Gold	Brass mitre
Poninski	10		Apple green	Apple green	Gold	
Granowski	11	Ostrogski Ordination	Black	Black	Gold	
Brühl		Artillery	Black	Black	Gold	N/A
Klein		Engineers	Black	Black	Silver	N/A
Poninski		Pontoneers	Red	Red	Silver	N/A

1776: Crown infantry independent companies

Unit	Jacket	Trim	Facings	Trousers	Hat
Grand Hetman Janissary	Red	White	Green	Red	White
Grand Hetman Hungarian	Green	Yellow	Red	Green	Black
Field Hetman Hungarian	Red	Yellow	Green	Red	Black
Grand Marshal Hungarian	Blue	Silver	Orange	White	Fusilier cap
Warsaw Militia	Light blue	Yellow	Light blue	Light blue	Black

1776: Grand Duchy of Lithuania infantry and technical corps

Chief	No.	Designation	Collar & cuffs	Lapels	Buttons	Grenadiers
Czartoryski		Guard	Blue	Blue	Gold	Bearskin
Oginski	1	Grand Hetman Grenadiers	White	White	Gold	Mitre
Oginski	2	Grand Hetman	Orange	Orange	Silver	Mitre
Sosnowski	3	Field Hetman	Black	Black	Gold	
Sosnowski	4	Field Hetman	Red	Red	Silver	
Grabowski	5	Grabowski	Yellow	Yellow	Silver	
Massalski	6	Xawery Niesolowski	Crimson	Crimson	Silver	
Stetkiewicz		Artillery	Black	Black	Gold	

1776: Grand Duchy of Lithuania infantry independent companies

Unit	Jacket	Trim	Facings	Trousers	Hat
Grand Hetman Janissary	Red	Black	Black	Red	Red
Field Hetman Janissary	Red	Green	Green	Red	Green
Grand Hetman Hungarian	Light blue	Yellow	Yellow	Light blue	Black
Field Hetman Hungarian	Light blue	Yellow		Light blue	Black

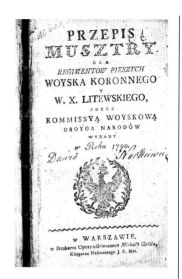

The first infantry manual for the Commonwealth forces was published in 1790, based on the Prussian manual. Apart from its technical content, it stressed service to the nation, rather than to a commander or local leaders.

The later 18th century had seen the evolution of the 'uniform *kontusz*', a more formal military jacket worn by senior officers with epaulettes and badges of rank, often over a white *zupan*. As part of the new regulations instituted in 1785, the *kontusz* was shortened for all ranks into the *kurtka* jacket that would become traditional for lancers in many armies; this was sometimes worn over a similarly shortened *zupanik* waistcoat. According to the ordinance of 27 February 1789, the Advance Guard units – employed, as their name implies, for scouting duties – had a different colour scheme: the *towarzycz* wore a green *kurtka* with regimentally-coloured facings, and green trousers. The cap was a crimson *konfederatka* with a white band above black lambswool edging, and white cords and plume.

The officers of the National Cavalry wore a blue, thigh-length, buttoned-across *litewka* jacket with crimson cuffs, collar and shoulder strap, crimson trousers with a yellow sidestripe, and silver and crimson belts. The trumpeters wore a scarlet *kurtka* with collar and lapels in blue, silver lace on the collar and cuffs, and yellow lace along the rear sleeve and body seams. Their scarlet trousers had white sidestripes; their mirliton had a blue-over-white plume, and white cords terminating in blue tassels. The saddle cloth was dark blue with the outer edge white (or silver) with a fringe, then (reading inwards) a red line, white, red and white. White or silver eagles embroidered in the rear corners were angled, with the eagle's crown pointing towards the rider. The pistol holster covers were in the same colours, with the king's crowned cypher in the centre.

The dragoon regiments were eventually converted into either infantry or Advance Guard cavalry units. Some retained their facing colours on infantry uniforms, and were inserted into the regimental seniority sequence; the Advance Guard units had blue or green jackets.

In the 1770s infantry uniforms retained their style and colours, with Crown troops in red coats and Duchy troops in blue. However, the 1780s were a decade of reforms; by the end of 1789 all infantry of both nations had adopted a standard uniform of a *kurtka* jacket and trousers in dark blue, with regimental distinctions at collar, cuffs, lapels, turnbacks, and trouser sidestripes.

Artillery continued to be clothed in infantry style, with green jackets faced in black.

The reforms of 1788 changed the colour of all equipment from Saxon red to green, with black iron fittings. However, in 1792 there were still gun carriages in Czestochowa that were painted red, and the ordered change was not completed until the end of the period. The royal cypher was painted on artillery equipment in white, along with the unit number.

General Sanguszko leading the 3rd Ukrainian Cavalry Bde of the Crown, 1792, in a painting by Juliusz Kossack (1871). The general is shown dressed according to the 1790 reforms, but his troopers in the background are still in their pre-1789 uniforms.

THE ARMY OF 1791–94

Organization

At the beginning of the 1792 War in Defence of the Constitution, Poland and Lithuania each had a general staff that consisted of a Grand Hetman, Field Hetman, general of artillery, lieutenant-general (divisional commander) and major-general.

1792: Crown cavalry

Chief	No.	Designation	Jacket	Facings	Buttons	Hat	Pennant
Potocki		Guard Dragoons	Red	Blue	Yellow	Black helmet	-
Mioduski	1	1st Wielkopolski	Blue	Crimson	Silver	Crimson	Red/white cross
Biernacki	2	2nd Wielkopolski	Blue	Crimson	Silver	Crimson	Red/white cross
Hadziewicz	3	1st Malopolski	Blue	Crimson	Silver	Crimson	Red/white cross
Manget	4	2nd Malopolski	Blue	Crimson	Silver	Crimson	Red/white cross
Swiejkowski	5	3rd Ukrainian	Blue	Crimson	Silver	Crimson	Red, single point
Jerlicz	6	2nd Ukrainian	Blue	Crimson	Red	Crimson	Red/white cross
Lubowidzki	7	1st Ukrainian	Blue	Crimson	Red	Crimson	Red/white cross
Sanguszko	8	4th Ukrainian	Blue	Red	Silver	Black	Red/white
Kening		King's Lancers	Green	Crimson	Gold	Crimson	Green/red/green/red
Szydlowski	1	Queen's Adv Gd	Blue	Crimson	Gold	Crimson	Crimson/blue/white fly with crimson Maltese cross
Zajaczek	2	Grand Hetman's Advance Guard	Green	Black	Gold	Red	Green/black
Zajaczek	3	Field Hetman's Advance Guard	Dark Green	Blue	Gold	Dark Green	Green/blue
Wurttemberg	4	Prince of Wurttemberg's Adv Guard	Blue	Red	Gold	Blue	Blue/red
Lubormirski	5	Advance Guard	Blue	Crimson	Gold	Crimson	Blue/red
		2nd King's Lancers	Green	Black	Gold	Red	Green/red
Potocki	1	Loyal Cossacks	Black	Red	-	Black	
Chomentowski	2	Loyal Cossacks	Black	White	-	Red	

1792: Grand Duchy of Lithuania cavalry

Chief	No	Designation	Jacket	Facings	Buttons	Hat	Pennant
Stryjenski		Horse Guards	Red	Blue	Gold	Black	
Ostrowski	1	Hussars of Kowienska Nat Cav Bde	Blue	Crimson	Gold	Crimson	Blue/red
Twardowski	2	Light Horse of Pinsk Nat Cav Bde	Blue	Crimson	Gold	Crimson	Blue/yellow
Kossakowski	3	National Cavalry Brigade	Blue	Crimson	Gold	Crimson	Blue/red
Kirkor	1	Advance Guard	Blue	Red	Gold	Red	Blue/red
Jelenski	2	Advance Guard	Blue	Red	Gold	Red	Blue/red
Chlewinski	3	Advance Guard	Blue	Red	Gold	Red	Blue/red
Bielak	4	Jozef Bielak Adv Guard	Blue	Red	Gold	Red	Blue/red
Byszewski	5	Stanislaw Byszewski Adv Guard	Blue	Red	Gold	Red	Blue/red
Azulewicz	6	2nd Nadworina Ulans	Red	Yellow	Silver	Red	Red/yellow
Ulan	7	Tartars	Red	Yellow	Silver	Red	Red/yellow

1792: Crown Infantry and technical corps

Chief	No.	Designation	Collar & cuffs	Lapels & turnbacks	Buttons
Poniatowski		Guards	Blue	Blue	Gold
Gorzenski	1	Queen Jadwiga	Crimson	Crimson	Gold
Wodzicki	2	Crown Prince	Crimson	Crimson	Silver
Czapski	3	Junior King	Green	Green	Silver
Branicki	4	Field Hetman	Green	Green	Silver
Rzewuski	5	Fusiliers	Black	Black	Gold
Ozarowski	6	Lanowy	Forest green	Forest green	Gold
Potocki	7		Cornflower blue	Cornflower blue	Gold
Rzewuski	8	Grand Hetman	Light blue	Light blue	Silver
Raczynski	9		Pink	Pink	Silver
Dzialynski	10		Yellow	Yellow	Gold
Illinski	11	Grenadiers	Yellow	Yellow	Gold
Lubormirski	12		Apple green	Apple green	Silver
Poninski	13	Ostrogski Ordination	Yellow	Yellow	Gold
Potocki	14		Light blue	Light blue	Silver
Cichocki	15		Black	Black	Gold
		Krakow Garrison	Black	Black	Silver
Marcia		Czestochowa Garrison	Black	Black	Silver
Potocki		Artillery	Black	Black	Gold
Potocki		Engineers	Black	Black	Silver
Kossowski		Pontoneers	Red	Red	Silver

1792: Grand Duchy of Lithuania infantry and technical corps

Chief	No.	Designation	Collar & cuffs	Lapels & turnbacks	Buttons
Jablonowski		Guard	Blue	Blue	Silver
Oginski	1	Grand Hetman Grenadiers	Red	Red	Gold
Oginski	2	Grand Hetman	Orange	Orange	Silver
Tyszkiewicz	3	Field Hetman	Green	Green	Gold
Judycki	4	Field Hetman	Turquoise	Turquoise	Silver
Grabowski	5	Grabowski	Light blue	Light blue	Silver
Niesiolowski	6	Xawery Niesolowski	Yellow	Yellow	Silver
Sapieha	7	Prince Sapieha	Black	Black	Silver
Radziwill	8	Radziwill Infantry	Black	Black	Silver
Radziwill	9		Black	Black	Silver
Kosielski		Artillery	Black	Black	Gold

1792: Grand Duchy of Lithuania infantry independent companies

Unit	Jacket	Trim	Facings	Trousers	Hat
Grand Hetman Hungarian	Light blue	Yellow	Yellow	Light blue	Black
Field Hetman Hungarian	Light blue	Yellow		Light blue	Black

17

Towarzycz of the 1st National Cavalry Bde, 1790, in watchcloak. The cloak is white, but the cape is in the colours of the uniform – crimson, collared and edged in blue. (Artist unknown, NAMW; author'scollection)

Obverse side of a standard of the 1st National Cavalry Bde (1st Wielkopolski); this design was common to cavalry in the period 1770–94, with the royal cypher 'SAR' on the reverse. The flag is of double-backed crimson silk damask, 55cm in the hoist and 60cm in the fly (21.6 x 23.6in), embroidered and fringed with gold. (NAMW; author's collection)

1792: Army of the Targowica Confederation

Cavalry					
Chief	a.k.a.	Jacket	Facings	Hat	Pennant
Borzecki	Kiev Hussars	Blue	Crimson	Crimson	Blue/red
Zlotnicki	Podolska Golden Liberty	Blue	Crimson	Crimson	Blue/red
Suchorzewski	Braclawice Hussars	Blue	Crimson	Crimson	Blue/red
Potocki	Humanski Light Cavalry	Blue	Crimson	Crimson	Blue/red
Leszczynski	Free Confederation Advance Guard	Blue	Crimson	Crimson	Blue/red

Infantry			
Chief	Jacket	Facings	Hat
Moszczewski	Infantry	Blue	Yellow	Blue

The cavalry brigades were commanded by brigadiers, seconded by a 'vice-brigadier' and a major. A captain (*rotmistrz*) commanded each 'banner' or squadron; the rank/appointment sequence below this was lieutenant, second lieutenant, quartermaster, auditor, adjutant, standard-bearer (ensign), deputy, comrade (*towarzycz*), sergeant-major, quartermaster NCO (comparable to the French rank of *fourrier*), corporal, and trooper (*pocztczowy*). By 1792 National Cavalry brigades consisted of 12 companies in the Crown and 16 in the Duchy armies; the brigades had a staff of 19 and 21 respectively, and companies had 150 troopers. Advance Guard regiments had a staff of 19, and 10 (Crown) and 8 (Duchy) companies, each of 135 troopers. The commander was the colonel, followed by a lieutenant-colonel, a major, and then the structure as in the cavalry brigades.

As part of the 1790 reforms, 10 or 12 men per battalion were selected as 'sharpshooters', and the following year these provided one company per regiment. In 1792 the Lithuanian sharpshooter companies were amalgamated into a Rifle Corps with four battalions, each of four companies, each company with a nominal strength of 147 soldiers. By 1794 at least one Crown regiment (the 19th) was designated as a rifle unit. Not all sharpshooters actually received rifled weapons.

The artillery was commanded by a major-general of artillery, seconded by a regimental colonel and lieutenant-colonel. Operationally, the artillery was dispersed by companies and batteries, usually being based in fortresses until needed in the field. The hierarchy in these operational units was a major in command, captain, quartermaster, adjutant, lieutenant, second lieutenant, artificer, staff quartermaster NCO, commissary, quartermaster NCO, master gunner, and gunner. Each infantry regiment had a 4-gun artillery battery attached to it, and soldiers were designated from the ranks of the regiment to serve these 2- or 3-pounder regimental guns. By 1792 artillery batteries had 6- or 12-pounder guns and 6in howitzers. The barrels were made of iron or bronze, but all carriages had iron furniture. The guns were usually towed behind wagons; by May 1792 there was a preliminary organization of some horse artillery units after the Prussian model. Gembarzewski shows horse artillery gunners from the Horse Guards regiment in 1794.

1794: Crown cavalry

Chief	No.	Designation	Jacket	Facings	Buttons	Hat	Pennant
Potocki		Guard Dragoons	Red	Blue	Yellow	Black	-
Madalinski	1	1st Wielkopolski	Blue	Crimson	Silver	Crimson	Red/white cross
Biernacki	2	2nd Wielkopolski	Blue	Crimson	Silver	Crimson	Red/white cross
Hadziewicz	3	1st Malopolski	Blue	Crimson	Silver	Crimson	Red/white cross
Manget	4	2nd Malopolski	Blue	Crimson	Silver	Crimson	Red/white cross
Swiejkowski	5	3rd Ukrainian	*to Russian army – Dniepiski Brigade*				
	6	2nd Ukrainian	*to Russian army – Dniestrzanski Bde*				
Lubowidzki	7	1st Ukrainian	*to Russian army – Braclawski Bde*				
	8	4th Ukrainian	*Disbanded*				
Wojciechowski		King's Lancers	Green	Crimson	Gold	Crimson	Green/red
Szydlowski	1	Queen's Adv Gd	Green	Crimson	Gold	Crimson	Crimson/blue/white fly, crimson Maltese cross
	2	Advance Guard	*to Russian army – Zytomirski Regt*				
Zajaczek	3	Advance Guard	Blue	Crimson	Gold	Crimson	Red/white/red/white
Byszewski	4	Advance Guard	*to Russian army – Konstantynowki Regt*				
Lubormirski	5	Advance Guard	*to Russian army – Iziastanski Regt*				
Joselewicz		Starozakonna Light Cavalry	Black	-	Silver	Black	
Krasicki		Hussars	Blue	Yellow	Gold	Black	

1794: Grand Duchy of Lithuania cavalry

Chief	No.	Designation	Jacket	Facings	Buttons	Hat	Pennant
Stryjenski		Horse Guards	Red	Blue	Gold	Black	
Ostrowski	1	Hussars of Kowienska Nat Cav Bde	Blue	Crimson	Gold	Crimson	Blue/red
Twardowski	2	Light Horse of Pinsk Nat Cav Bde	Blue	Crimson	Gold	Crimson	Blue/yellow
Kossakowski	3	National Cavalry Brigade	Blue	Crimson	Gold	Crimson	Blue/red
Kirkor	1	Advance Guard	*to Russian army – Lithuanian-Tartar Regt*				
Kadlubinski	2	Advance Guard	Blue	Red	Gold	Red	Blue/red
Piruski	3	Advance Guard	Blue	Red	Gold	Red	Blue/red
Bielak	4	Jozef Bielak Adv Guard	Blue	Red	Gold	Red	Blue/red
Lissowski	5	Stanislaw Byszewski Adv Guard	Blue	Red	Gold	Red	Blue/red
Achmatowicz	6	2nd Nadwornych Ulans	Blue	Red	Gold	Red	Red/yellow
Ulan	7	Tartars	Dark blue	Red	Silver	Red	Red/blue
Weyssenhoff	8		Blue	Red	Gold	Red	Blue/red

The Corps of Engineers and Pontoneers was headed by a 'Chief'; subordinate ranks were colonel, lieutenant-colonel, captain, lieutenant, second lieutenant, conductor, under-officer, miner and sapper.

Uniforms

The ordinance of March 1791 was the final set of uniform regulations issued to the army that would fight the Russians in 1792 and 1794.

In the cavalry the height of the *konfederatka* was lowered. In the National Cavalry the *pocztowy* was given a black cylindrical mirliton (*giwer*) with a white plume and cords; this was about 20cm (8in) high, sometimes

Trooper (*pocztowy*) of the 1st National Cavalry Bde, 1790; see Plate F2. He wears the distinguishing headgear of his rank, a felt mirliton or *giwer*, dressed with white cords and a white-over-black plume. These troopers served in the rear ranks and carried swords and firearms, but usually not lances; note the carbine or short musket with a visible slinging-rail. (Artist unknown, NAMW; author's collection)

with a fold-up visor and neck flap. The *kurtka* was dark blue with crimson distinctions, the trousers crimson with a blue stripe. In the Advance Guard, the *pocztowy* wore the same mirliton but with a white-over-black plume, while the *towarzycz* wore the *konfederatka*. The *kurtkas* in these regiments were either green or blue; collar and cuffs were black, lapels were crimson, and buttons, lace and epaulettes were gold. The trousers were crimson with black stripes. The Crown Guard Dragoons wore a round black leather 'Tarleton'-style helmet with a visor and crest, sometimes with a cloth turban, a pointed brass frontal plate, a horsehair mane and brass chinscales. Their *kurtka* was red with blue distinctions, their trousers blue with a red stripe, but otherwise their uniform was in the new regulation style. The Lithuanian Guard cavalry seem to have retained the dragoon-style bicorne hat, but with the revised uniform.

In 1791 a shako (*casquet*) was introduced for the Crown infantry units. This incorporated elements of design from similar caps worn in the Austrian, Prussian and Russian armies, but was uniquely Polish in its final form. It was of black felt with leather details, with a flat top, a separate front flap with a white metal plate featuring a Polish eagle, an upright plume on the left side, and a black moose-hair or fur crest or roach on a wire former; this rose from low on the back and up over the top to the front flap. Prior to 1792, and after 1794, Polish infantry regiments included a grenadier component, but regulations from that era seem silent on this subject. It would be logical that they were still an organic part of the regiment, and were distinguished by a sideways shako crest (like Prussian and Russian grenadiers during this period). In the iconography some troops within units are shown with sideways crests in white, but these are unexplained.

Soldiers from the 2nd Crown Foot Regt 'Crown Prince' (Wodzicki's), 1790–94 – see Plate E1. Note the transverse crest, in what has been called the 'grenadier' style, although this explanation is only speculative. In this drawing of 1812 the artist Michal Stachowicz has wrongly depicted the 1791 Polish *casquets* as if they were Austrian shakos, and the frontal turnbacks on the *kurtka* jacket are too small. (Author's collection)

1794: Crown infantry and technical corps

Chief	No.	Designation	Collar & cuffs	Lapels & turnbacks	Buttons
Poniatowski		Guards	Blue	Blue	Gold
Gorzenski	1	Queen Jadwiga	Pink	Pink	Gold
Wodzicki	2	Crown Prince	Pink	Pink	Silver
Czapski	3	Junior King	Green	Green	Silver
Branicki	4	Field Hetman	Green	Green	Silver
Rzewuski	5	Fusiliers	Black	Black	Gold
Ozarowski	6	Lanowy	Forest green	Forest green	Gold
Potocki	7		Cornflower blue	Cornflower blue	Gold
Rzewuski	8	Grand Hetman	to Russian army – Kamienets Musketeer Regt		
Raczynski	9		Pink	Pink	Silver
Dzialynski	10		Yellow	Yellow	Gold
Illinski	11	Grenadiers	to Russian army – Mohylewski Musketeer Regt		
Lubormirski	12		to Russian army – Izialav Grenadier Regt		
Poninski	13	Ostrogski Ordination	Yellow	Yellow	Gold
Potocki	14		disbanded		
Cichocki	15		Black	Black	Gold
Gislier	16	Treasury	Black	Black	Gold
Rottenburg	17		Black	Black	Gold
Krasinski	18		Black	Black	Gold
Sokolnicki	19	Riflemen	Green	Green	Silver
Kilinski	20		Red	Red	Gold
Paszkowski	21	Podlaski Pikemen	Black	Black	Gold
		Krakow Garrison	Black	Black	Silver
		Volunteer Infantry	Yellow	Yellow	Silver
Potocki		Artillery	Black	Black	Gold
Potocki		Engineers	Black	Black	Silver
Kossowski		Pontoneers	Red	Red	Silver

1794: Grand Duchy of Lithuania infantry and technical corps

Chief	No.	Designation	Collar & cuffs	Lapels & turnbacks	Buttons
Jablonowski		Guard	Blue	Blue	Silver
Oginski	1	Grand Hetman Grenadiers	Red	Red	Gold
Oginski	2	Grand Hetman	Orange	Orange	Silver
Tyszkiewicz	3	Field Hetman	Green	Green	Gold
Judycki	4	Field Hetman	Turquoise	Turquoise	Silver
Grabowski	5	Grabowski	Light blue	Light blue	Silver
Niesiolowski	6	Xawery Niesolowski	Yellow	Yellow	Silver
Sapieha	7	Prince Sapieha	Black	Black	Silver
Radziwill	8	Radziwill Infantry	Black	Black	Silver
Radziwill	9		Black	Black	Silver
Kosielski		Artillery	Black	Black	Gold
Sapieha		Engineers	Black	Black	Gold

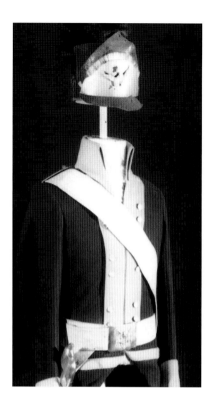

Lithuanian infantry received a helmet similar in outline to the *Raupenhelm* adopted by Bavaria a few years later. This was of black felt, with a domed top and a black bearskin crest from halfway up the back to the top. A plate featuring the Polish eagle or the Lithuanian armoured horseman was fixed to the front above a brass band.

The artillery, engineers and pontoneers continued to wear green *kurtkas* with black facings and trim, and the headgear of their respective army.

UNITS OF THE POLISH CROWN AND GRAND DUCHY OF LITHUANIA, 1765–94

Key: *(F)* = date of raising or formation; *(S)* = where known to have been stationed; *(B)* = battles/actions where known to have been present – or, if individual battle history uncertain, then e.g. 'Bar civil war' or '1792 War' = took part in this conflict. This listing is not comprehensive, but represents those units that we have identified with colonels-in-chief and uniform distinctions applicable to the reign of Stanislaw II August. For colonels-in-chief at key dates, see also the tables in this book.

Even though some units were incorporated into the Russian army under the Second Partition, the Polish command tried to raise new troops to fill those regimental numbers in the Line, and these would have been uniformed like their predecessors. This explains some apparent contradictions in the summaries of regimental participation in engagements during 1794.

CROWN CAVALRY

Guard Cavalry of the Crown Also known as (a.k.a.) the Mirowska Dragoons; incorporated a Cossack contingent. In addition, at different dates hussar and *pancerni* companies were also attached to the King's Guard. The regiment was stationed in Warsaw and Krakow; it saw active service from the Bar Confederation War until the end of the Warsaw Insurrection, and in 1794 fought in the battles at Slonima, Krupczyce, Brzesc and Maciejowice.

In 1760–89 the Crown Guard Dragoons were dressed like their Saxon forebears, in tricorne hat, buff-coloured coat and breeches, and high-topped black boots. They had red turnbacks, and white (silver) lace trim; for full dress they wore a red tabard in imitation of a cuirass. The saddle cloth was crimson with silver edges and a silver Polish eagle in the rear corners.

From 1790 to 1795 the unit adopted red jackets with blue facings and gold buttons. The headgear now resembled the visored, crested 'Tarleton' or 'Rumford'-style leather helmet that was internationally fashionable for light cavalry. Some had a cloth turban around the base, and a horsehair mane hanging from the raised comb. Bacciarelli shows Prince Jozef Poniatowski (the King's nephew) in uniform as commander of the Guards in a buff coat with blue distinctions, a light dragoon helmet with a leopardskin turban, a breastplate, and buff breeches. The saddle cloth was crimson with triple gold lace edging, and a crowned royal cypher in silver angled in the rear corners.

1st Brigade of National Cavalry (1st Wielkopolski) *(F)* 1776, from hussar and *pancerni* 'banners' from Wielkopolska; at end of 1789 constituent companies were numbered from 1 to 24. *(S)* Szrensk, Rypin, Raciaz, Sulmierzyce, Stawiszyn, Pyzdry, Gniezno (1792), Ryczywoł, Kolo, Pultusk (1794), Ostrolenka. *(B)* Szrensk, Wyszogrod, Lowicz, Stara Rawa, Rawa, Inowlodz, Konskie, Raclawice, Szczekociny, Starczyska, Warsaw, Golkow, Czerniakow and Lachy (1794).

Leib=Regiment Dragoner en Parade in Super Weste und Collet.

Przedny Straz. 1te Pułk Comend: Gener: Biszewski.

Towarzycz and *pocztowy* of Luba's 1st National Cavalry Bde (1st Wielkopolski), 1783. The uniforms are blue faced with crimson, and the 'comrade's' distinctions include aiguillettes, an epaulette, yellow boots, and sabre slings. The origin of the common trooper's taller, quilted cap could be traced to a tradional Tartar style. (Gabriel Raspe, NAMW; courtesy of Arsenal.org.pl)

2nd Brigade of National Cavalry (2nd Wielkopolski) *(F)* Nov 1789. *(S)* Warta, Kozienice (1792), Koscian, Przedborz (1793), Checiny, Wlodzimierz (1794), Kowel. *(B)* Zielence, Dubniki, Dubienka (1792); Szczekociny, Warsaw, Zbaraz, Raclawice (1794).

3rd Brigade of National Cavalry (1st Malopolski) *(F)* 1789. *(S)* Wislica, Stobnica, Nowe Miasto (1790), Sandomierz (1792), Bielsk (1792), Brianska, Lomza. *(B)* Zielence (1792); Stanislawa, Chelm, Uscilugie, Warsaw, Goluchow, Witkowice, Strzyze, Maciejowice (1794).

4th Brigade of National Cavalry (2nd Malopolski) *(F)* 1789. *(S)* Augustow (1790), Wolyn (8 banners) & Mazowiecki (4 banners) (1792); Warsaw, Solca. *(B)* Granne, Opatowie (1792); Kozubow, Raclawice, Szczekociny, Warsaw, Sielce, Rzewnie, Karniewkie, Gzowo, Strzyze (1794).

5th Brigade of National Cavalry (3rd Ukrainian) *(F)* 1776, from hussar and *pancerni* banners from Ukraine; 1789, companies numbered 42–72. *(S)* Bialocerkiew, Mohylew, Targowica & (8 banners) Malopolska (1779–82). *(B)* Motowilowka, Boruszkowce, Zielence, Dubienka (1792). Transferred into Russian army (1793) as Dniepiski Bde.

6th Brigade of National Cavalry (2nd Ukrainian) *(F)* as 5th Bde above; 1789, companies numbered 73–96. *(S)* Bialocerkiew, Labunie (1779), Mohylow, Zwaniec, Tulczyn (1789), Janowiec -on- Wisla (1792), Dniepre (1793). *(B)* Serby, Nowa Sieniawka, Zielence, Bereza, Markuszow (1792). Transferred into Russian army (1793) as Dniestrzanski Bde.

7th Brigade of National Cavalry (1st Ukrainian) *(F)* 1776, from hussar and *pancerni* banners from Ukraine and Podlaskie; 1789, companies numbered 25–48. *(S)* Szarogrod (1776–92), Zwinogrod (1792). *(B)* Serby, Cekinowka, Morafa, Zielence, Dubienka (1792). Transferred into Russian army (1793) as Braclawski Bde; but listed in action at Bialoreka, Stary Konstantynow, Wlodzimierz, Chelm, Goluchow, Raszyn, Wola, Powazek, Warsaw (1794).

8th Brigade of National Cavalry (4th Ukrainian) *(F)* 1789. *(S)* Human, Bohopol-Czehryn, Granne & Jampol (1792). *(B)* Zaslawa, Wiszniopola, Boruszkowce, Zielence (1792). Transferred into Russian army (1793) as Wolynski Bde; but listed at Bialoreka, Warsaw, Sochaczew, Blonie, Powazki, Gorce, Szymanow, Wiskitki, Tokar, Witkowice, Zukow, Kamionna, Bzura (1794).

Kossak's painting of Eustachy Sanguszko's regiment in 1792 seems to show an older cavalry uniform: a blue *kontusz* with crimson cuffs, over a crimson *zupan* and blue trousers. The headgear is a black *kolpak* with a red bag and white feather, and the lance pennant is red-over-white. A trumpeter has a red jacket with light blue collar, cuffs and turnbacks, and light blue trousers with a white sidestripe; he wears a black mirliton with white cords. The horse blanket is shown as red with light blue edging.

1st 'Queen's' Regiment of the Crown Advance Guard *(F)* 1789, from dragoons. *(S)* Cudnow, Powolocz, Warsaw. *(B)* Burakowski Karczmie, Raczki, Boruszkowe, Zielence (1792); Warsaw, Szczekociny, Strzyze, Praga (1794).

2nd Regiment of the Crown Advance Guard (Grand Hetman's) *(F)* 1789, from dragoons. *(S)* Mohylow, Chwasta, Czeczelnik. *(B)* Zielence, Wlodzimierz (1792); transferred into Russian army (1793) as Zytomirski Regt. In 1790 the troopers' saddle cloth was black with red trim, for *towarzycz* and officers it was red with white.

3rd Regiment of the Crown Advance Guard (Field Hetman's) *(F)* 1789, from dragoons. *(S)* Luck, Chmielnik, Kowel (1792). *(B)* Zielence, Dubienka (1792); Chelm, Uscilug, Warsaw, Powazek (1794).

(continued on page 33)

1

3

2

A

CAVALRY, 1770s
1: *Towarzycz* of Crown Hussars, *c.*1770
2: *Pocztowy* of National Cavalry, 1776
3: *Towarzycz*, 2nd Lithuanian Advance
Guard Regt (Jelenski's), late 1770s

B

INFANTRY, 1770s
1: Janissary Company of Grand Hetman of the Crown, 1770
2: Grenadier NCO, Lithuanian Footguard Regt (Czartoryski's), 1775
3: Musketeer, 1st Crown Foot Regt 'Queen Jadwiga' (Golcz's), 1779

C

CROWN GUARDS, 1790s
1: Musketeer, Crown Footguard Regt
(Poniatowski's), 1792
2: Dragoon, Crown Guard Dragoons
(Potocki's), 1792
3: Gunner, Crown Guard Horse Artillery,
1794

LINE INFANTRY, 1790s
1: Musketeer, 2nd Crown Foot Regt 'Crown Prince' (Wodzicki's)
2: Musketeer, 5th Lithuanian Foot Regt (Grabowski's)
3: Rifleman, 10th Crown Foot Regt (Dzialynski's)

E

NATIONAL CAVALRY, 1790s
1: Officer, 1st National Cavalry Brigade
2: *Pocztowy*, 1st National Cavalry Brigade
3: *Towarzycz*, 2nd Crown Advance Guard
Regt, 1792

PEASANT MILITIA; RACLAWICE, 1794
1: Scytheman, Krakow 'Grenadiers'
2: Musketeer, Sandomierz 'Grenadiers'
3: Militia cavalryman

G

In 1789 the saddle cloth was dark blue with red edging. In 1794 the trumpeters wore a red *giwer* with a white plume tipped red; white jackets with blue facings edged gold, and gold and red shoulder straps edged gold; trousers were red with a white sidestripe. The saddle cloth was dark blue, edged in gold with a red central stripe; the pistol holsters was edged in gold only.

4th Regiment of the Crown Advance Guard *(F)* 1776, from light cavalry. *(S)* Warta, Czehryn (1792). *(B)* as Prince of Wurttemberg's Regt at Izabelina (1792). Transferred into Russian army (1793) as Konstantynowski Regt; but listed at Mscibow, Brzesc, Skalmierz, Raclawice, Warsaw, Szczekociny, Chelm and Krupczyce (1794).

Up to 1789 the musicians had gold lace on their sleeves and 'swallow's-nest' shoulder wings, and the saddle cloth was green with red edging and gold eagles. In 1794, trumpeters had a white jacket with black distinctions, red trousers with a yellow sidestripe, a black mirliton with a white plume tipped red, and a red over-sash edged in gold. The saddle cloth was blue, with white and red edging separated by a gold line.

5th Regiment of the Crown Advance Guard *(F)* 1776, from light cavalry. *(S)* Tetyow, Berszadie (1787), Czeczelnik (1789), Wisniowiec. *(B)* as Prince Lubormirski's Regt at Wisznioploa, Boruszkowce, Zielence (1792). Transferred into Russian army (1793) as Izajaslawski (Zaslawski) Regt; but listed at Szczekociny, Warsaw, Blonie, Czerniakow, Krupczyce, Brzesc and Maciejowice (1794).

1st Regiment of Loyal Cossacks *(F)* May 1792, from western Cossacks, under Maj Jan Potocki of National Cavalry; Oct 1792, became Kiev Light Cavalry Regt of Targowica Confederation.

In 1792 the unit wore a black lambswool cap with a red bag, a black *kontusz* trimmed with white piping, and black trousers with a yellow sidestripe piped each side with white. Under the *kontusz* was a red *zupan*, also piped in white along the pointed cuffs and down-turned collar. They wore a crimson sash, and black boots. The lance had no pennant. A brown camelhair *burqa* was worn over the shoulders in bad weather.

2nd Regiment of Loyal Cossacks *(F)* May 1792 by Prince Czartoryski, with recruits from Berzadski, Korsunski and Granowski. First colonel Prince Jozef Poniatowski, replaced June 1792 by Michal Chomentowski. Became part of Kiev Light Cavalry Regt of Targowica Confederation, and eventually Bohski Light Cavalry Regt of Russian army.

They wore a red *kuczma* with black lambswool edging. The black *kontusz* and trousers were piped white, the yellow trouser sidestripe being piped white each side. Under the *kontusz* they wore a red *zupan*, piped white along the pointed cuffs and down-turned collar. Their sash was crimson, their boots black, and they had no lance pennant.

King's Lancer Regiment This unit, which could trace its origins to the 17th century, was the first to be designated a Lancer regiment. *(S)* Warsaw, Lomazy (1774), Korsun (1787), Kozienice (1794). *(B)* Bar civil war; Warsaw, Nowy Dwory, Slonim, Zegrze, Krupczyce, Brzesc, Maciejowicie, Praga (1794).

CROWN DRAGOONS

Queen's Dragoon Regiment *(F)* 1717; became 1st Advance Guard Regt (qv) during 1789 reforms. *(S)* Krakow, Sandomierz, Labun (1777), Cudnow (1778).

Prince's Dragoon Regiment *(F)* early 18th C; (1733–63) named Prince's Horse Regt of HM Prince Frederick; 1789, became 8th Foot Regt (qv) of Antoni Czapski. *(S)* Pomorskie (1717), Poznan (1763), Lowicz (1775).
Grand Hetman's Horse Regiment *(F)* early 18th C; 1789, became 2nd Advance Guard Regt of Grand Hetman (qv). *(S)* Lwow, Wolynskie, Belzyce, Podlaski, Pomorskie (1717), Luboml.
Field Hetman's Horse Regiment *(F)* early18th C; 1789, became 3rd Advance Guard Regt (qv). *(S)* Podhorce & Strzelno (1775), Tetyow (1779).
Raczynski Foundation Dragoon Regiment *(F)* 1717, as Podlaski Horse; 1776, became dragoon regt; 1789, became 9th Foot Regt (qv). *(S)* Wielkopolska, Lowicz (1777).
Dismounted Dragoon Regiment *(F)* early 18th C; 1776, became dragoon regt; 1789, became 7th Foot Regt (qv). *(S)* Miedzyrzec (1764), Koscian (1775). *(B)* Ukraine rebellions (1768–69), Bar civil war.

CROWN CAVALRY FORMED 1794

Starozakonna Light Cavalry Regiment, a.k.a. Jewish Light Cavalry Regt (*lekkokonny pułk żydowski*) *(F)* 1794 in Praga district, Warsaw. In the 18th century Jews were exempt from conscription into the Commonwealth forces, but a Jewish merchant named Joseph Aronowicz approached Kosciuszko to authorize this unit. Raised in Sept–Oct 1794 under Col Berek Joselewicz, it was designated a dragoon unit, and eventually reached a strength of 500. *(B)* Maciejowicie, and Praga, where most of the troopers were killed.
Volunteer Cavalry of 1794 One unit of volunteer horse shown by Norbin wore a green dolman and trousers with black boots and belts. Facings and piping (including a trouser stripe) were red, and buttons brass; the black *giwer* had white cords and plume. For peasant militia cavalry, see Plate G3.
Hussar Detachment Reported moving in Sept 1794 from Warsaw to Galicia, under the command of Maj J. Krasicki. They wore a blue hussar uniform with yellow/ochre distinctions: collar, cuffs, and double lacing between 15 brass front buttons, Hungarian knots above the cuffs and on the thighs. The pelisse was yellow/ochre with 2in-wide black fur on the cuffs and edges, and black lace across the front and on the collar. The sabretache was yellow/ochre with dark blue trim, with the word 'Jednosc' written diagonally across the length. The belting was white.

CROWN INFANTRY

Foot Guard Regiment of the Crown One of the oldest units in the army, stationed in Warsaw. It was originally titled *Das Hochlössliche Königliche Polnische Kron-Guardes Infanterie Regiment* – reflecting the German identity of the monarchy during the early 18th century. In 1794 the regiment fought at and around Warsaw, at Powazki, Gorce, Zegrze, Powazki, Karczma Welanski, Krupczyce, Brzesc, Maciejowice and Praga.
1st Crown Foot Regiment 'Queen Jadwiga' One of the oldest regiments after the Foot Guards, named by King Stanislaw August after his patroness. *(S)* Poznan (1775), Kalisz (1785), Winnica (1788), Piotrkow (1789), Stary Konstantynow (1791), Kalisz, Pleszew (Oct 1792), Parczew (1793). *(B)* 1792 War.

The regimental flag of the Foot Guards, 1770–94; two flags were carried, one with a crimson field and one white, measuring 140cm in the hoist by 155cm in the fly (55 x 61in). On the reverse was a crimson circle in four quadrants separated by silver. The Polish eagle, first and third, was gold; the Lithuanian armoured rider, second and fourth, was in colours. On the obverse was the royal cypher 'SAR' in silver, 55cm (21.6in) high. The laurel leaves were green, the crown gold, and the ribbons blue and white. The brass spearhead finial measured 26cm (10.25in), on a black shaft 274cm (107.8in) long. (From Anusiewicz; author's collection)

2nd Crown Foot Regiment 'Crown Prince' *(F)* by King August III in name of his son Crown Prince Karol; retained number 2 in Line until after Kosciuszko Insurrection. *(S)* Kamieniec, Poznan, Krakow (1775). *(B)* Bar civil war; 1792 War as Wodzicki's Regiment; 1794, two battalions fought at Raclawice, including rifle company.

3rd Crown Foot Regiment Originally Prince's Dragoon Regiment. Joined Line infantry as 8th Regt; 1790, its Chief Nikolaj Czapski had it advanced to 3rd, which place it retained in1792 and 1794. A.k.a. King's Junior Regt, and Czapski's Grenadier Regt. *(S)* Lowicz & Jozefow (1777), Radom (1779), Warsaw (1780), Radom & Kielce (1789), Krakow (1794). *(B)* 1792 War; 1794, two battalions plus riflemen fought at Raclawice.

In 1791–94 drummers had blue jackets with white chevron lace on sleeves, and a helmet with a red crest. Drums were brass, with red-and-white 'toothed' borders. Soldiers had red facings and trouser sidestripes, and white leather equipment; officers had silver epaulettes. The sharpshooters wore black broad-brimmed hats with a green plume, with regulation jacket and trousers and black leather equipment. Stachowicz shows riflemen in blue rather than green uniforms, with yellow sidestripes, black leatherwork and white hat plume.

4th Crown Foot Regiment 'Field Hetman' *(F)* 1726. *(S)* Bialystok & Lwow (1771), Kamieniec (1775), Leczna (1778), Bialocerkiew & Lubomla (1794). Fought in 1792 War, and at Szczekociny (1794).

5th Crown Regiment of Fusiliers Traditionally claimed to date from King Jan III Sobieski's Vienna campaign (1683); 1717, numbered 5th in seniority. The nominal Chief was the General of Artillery of the Crown, since its mission was to guard the artillery. In 1775, Fusilier Regt of Crown Artillery retitled Fusilier Battalion; 1776, listed as 5th Regt of Fusiliers; 1788, renumbered 6th in the Line; 1789, reverted to original name; 1792, reverted to 5th. *(S)* Kamieniec Podolski, Bialystok (1776), Warsaw; April 1794, two companies Warsaw, remainder Chelm. *(B)* Boruszkowce, Zielence, Dubienka (1792); Slonim, Krupczyce, Terespol, Maciejowice (1794).

Sharpshooters wore light green uniform with black distinctions, but white leatherwork; black round hats, black half-boots.

6th Crown Foot Regiment of Lanowy *(F)* 1726, as Lanowy (King's Landed Peasantry) Regt, traditionally associated with Crown Estates Militia. Originally the Guard Lanowy (*Gwardia Lanowy*) when numbered 6th in the Line, it was briefly the 9th (1790), and 7th (1791), reverting to 6th in 1792. *(S)* Kamieniec Podolski, Wschowa, Warsaw (1775), Wschowa (1779), Wlodzimierz (1790), Wolbrom (1790), Wschowa (1792). Took part in 1792 War and 1794 Insurrection.

7th Crown Foot Regiment *(F)* 1776, as dismounted dragoon regt; 1789, became 'Inf Regt of Col Potocki, *Starosta* of Szczerzecki' under Piotr Franciszek Potocki, later a member of the Targowica Confederation. Originally numbered 7th; then 8th (1790–92); then 9th; and reverted to 7th in 1794 Insurrection. *(S)* Kalisz, Poznan (1786), Lowicz (1790). *(B)* 1792 War.

8th Crown Foot Regiment 'Grand Hetman' *(F)* 1717, originally numbered 3rd, then 5th, and finally 8th; its colonel-in-chief was always the Grand Hetman of the Crown Armies. *(S)* Kamieniec Podolski. Ceased to exist 2 May 1793 under Second Partition, after which transferred into Russian army as Kamienets Musketeer Regt.

Infantry regimental flag, 1788–94. It is possible that two flags were carried, one crimson and the other white, as in the Guards. Known examples are 136cm in the hoist by 174cm in the fly (53.3 x 68.3in), and 154cm by 172cm (60.6 x 67.7in). The central silver eagle was 56cm high by 60cm wide (22 x 23.6in); the crown and laurels were both gold, and the ribbons blue. On the obverse was the crowned, wreathed cypher as on the Guards flag, but 59cm high (23.2in). The black-painted shaft measured 270.5cm (106.8in) long. (From Anusiewicz; author's collection)

Infantry soldier of 1794, wearing an overcoat and carrying a knapsack of unshaved animal hide. Note the somewhat shabby *casquet* shako, here without a back-to-front crest, and with both the peak and a rear flap turned upwards. (Aleksander Orlowski, NAMW)

Militia fusilier, 1794 – either a peasant or a villager. He has a comfortable cap and an overcoat, and has apparently been issued regulation crossbelt equipment. On his back he seems to carry a bundled and tied blanket as a knapsack. (Aleksander Orlowski, NAMW)

Warsaw Hungarian Company, 1781. The cap is similar to that of contemporary fusiliers; the officer's plume is white, the soldier's red. The officer is shown with a black stock, the soldier with a red one. The coats are sky blue, faced red and lined white. Hungarian companies were raised by particular commanders, since at that time they evoked an elite image – comparable to that of Zouaves in the mid 19th century. (Gabriel Raspe, NAMW; courtesy of Arsenal.org.pl)

9th Crown Foot Regiment *(F)* 1776, as Raczynski Foundation Dragoon Regt, by Filip Nereusz Raczynski. 1789, 9th Crown Foot Regt; 1790, briefly 10th; by 1792, again 9th. *(S)* Lowicz (1777–92), Warsaw, Poznan. *(B)* 1792 War; one battalion fought at Raclawice (1794).

10th Crown Foot Regiment (Rydzynski Ordination) *(F)* 1775 by August Sulkowski, Voivode of Kalisz, from his private militia; received royal patent 27 Nov 1776. 1789, renumbered 11th; 1794, reverted to 10th. Last colonel-in-chief was Ignacy Dzialynski, and unit later known by his name. *(S)* Rydzyna, Warsaw (1789), Gniezno (1790), Krakow (1794). *(B)* 1792 War; Maciejowice (1794). The sharpshooters wore green uniform with yellow facings, and round hat with green plume.

11th Crown Foot Regiment of Grenadiers *(F)* 1775 by Prince Jerzy Lubomirski from private militia. 1776, reduced to two battalions, one stationed in Kamieniec and the other in Lubar; fomer retained the title Grenadier Regt, while the latter remained in Lubormirski's private army. 1779, Grenadier Regt came under command of Maj Janusz Ilinski of the artillery. 1788–89, numbered as the 10th, and briefly in 1790 as the 12th, but by that April finally as the 11th. *(B)* 1792 War; May 1793, transferred into Russian army as Mohylewski Musketeer Regt.

12th Crown Foot Regiment *(F)* 1775 by Kalikst Poninski. 1778, admitted to army rolls as 12th in the Line; 1790, briefly renumbered 13th. *(S)* Kozmin, Kamieniec (1778), Labun (1785), Tulczyn (1789). *(B)* 1792 War; May 1793, transferred into Russian army as Izjaslawski (Izialav) Grenadier Regt. According to Nafziger, this was one of a number of former Polish regiments that were disbanded in 1794 because of the Kosciuszko Insurrection.

13th Foot Regiment (Ostrogski Ordination) *(F)* 1609, under Prince Janusz Ostrogski. After 1776, taken onto the army rolls as 13th Line; 1790, briefly renumbered 14th. *(S)* Dubno. *(B)* 1792 War and 1794 Insurrection.

14th Crown Foot Regiment *(F)* 1785 by Szczesny Potocki from his peasants, issued equipment from his private army. 1786, enrolled in Crown forces as 14th Line; 1790, briefly renumbered 7th. *(S)* Tulczyn. *(B)* 1792 War. When ordered transferred to Russia following Second Partition, the soldiers deserted to Turkish territory.

15th Crown Foot Regiment *(F)* 1792 by the Great Sejm in anticipation of war with Russia. *(S)* Warsaw. Disbanded, but re-formed before 1794 Insurrection around cadre from Foot Guard Regt. *(B)* Ostrolenka, Zegrze, Krupczyce, Terespol, Warsaw, Maciejowice, Praga (1794). In 1794 its rifle element wore black round hats with green plume, green uniform with red distinctions, and black leatherwork.

16th Crown Foot Regiment (Treasury) *(F)* 1794, from 250 Treasury militiamen, plus Crown Pioneer Corps, Lithuanian Crown Lands militia and Pontoneer Corps; 1,000-plus strong late that year. *(S)* Warsaw. *(B)* Zegrze, Maciejowice, Praga.

17th Crown Foot Regiment *(F)* April 1794, from Masovian volunteers. *(S)* Warsaw.

18th Crown Foot Regiment *(F)* April 1794, in part from soldiers discharged from 5th Fusiliers. *(S)* Warsaw; one battalion served in Nadnarwianski Division. *(B)* Wasosz, Okrzeja, Chelm, Stawiska, Krupczyce, Brzesc, Maciejowice.

19th Crown Foot Regiment of Riflemen *(F)* April 1794 by Michal Sokolnicki, Commander of Wielkopolska. *(S)* Warsaw. *(B)* Marymont, Krupczyce, Brzesc.

20th Crown Foot Regiment *(F)* 1794 under Jan Kilinski; part of Warsaw garrison.

21st Crown Foot Regiment *(F)* May 1794 as Podlaskie Pikemen Regt; Sept, retitled 21st Foot. *(S)* Warsaw. *(B)* against Prussians at Koln, Slosarza, Ostroleka.

1st Regiment of Krakow Grenadiers One of the regiments formed after the battle of Raclawice (April 1794) from peasants of the Krakow region, given the honorific title 'Grenadiers' to recognize their courageous contribution to that victory while armed in the great majority with only scythes and pikes.

2nd Regiment of Krakow Grenadiers See above.

Regiment of Lublin Grenadiers *(F)* May 1794.

Regiment of Sandomierz Grenadiers *(F)* April 1794.

Independent units:

Janissary Company of the Grand Hetman of the Crown The company existed from 1717 to 1775 under the command of the Grand Hetman. *(S)* wherever the Grand Hetman had his headquarters. *(B)* Bar civil war. For uniform *c.*1770–89, see Plate C1.

Hungarian Company of the Grand Hetman of the Crown The company existed from 1717 to 1789, then again in 1793. In 1764 they wore a light blue braided dolman with gold lace and yellow cuffs (red for officers). The tight Hungarian breeches were light blue, and officers had gold Hungarian knots embroidered on the thighs. All ranks wore a red sash. The enlisted men wore a black mirliton, while for officers this had a 'flame' or 'wing' and white feathers at the front. They are pictured with a red *delia* – a sort of fur-lined coat/cloak, traditionally worn over a *zupan*. In 1775–89 a new uniform was worn.

Hungarian Company of the Field Hetman of the Crown This also existed from 1717 to 1789, and again in 1793.

(Warsaw) Hungarian Company of the Grand Marshal of the Crown This company existed during the same periods as above. *(B)* Warsaw uprising (1794). See illustration opposite.

Miscellaneous Crown troops

Garrison of Krakow In 1794 they are pictured by Stachowicz wearing the regulation shako, but with a white transverse crest.

Warsaw Militia 1760s: Light blue jackets with yellow/buff turnbacks, over either a *zupan* or a waistcoat in yellow/buff; light blue trousers; either black tricorne or fur *kolpak*. 1794: Local militias had partly civilian and partly military clothing; prevalent headgear seems to have been a stovepipe hat, 'liberty cap' or *konfederatka*.

Volunteers of 1794 Many of these small operational units wore either a broad-brimmed round hat, sometimes with the left brim pinned up, or a black *giwer* with a white plume. One sketch by Norblin shows a grey three-quarter-length overcoat lined with white. The *sukmana* peasant overcoat was usually white but sometimes brown or blue (see Plate G).

Scythemen of the Krakow Grenadiers, 1794, as depicted by Michal Stachowicz in 1812 (and see Plate G). Their crimson standard bears a *rogatywka* cap above a cornsheaf and leafy branches, set against a crossed pike and scythe. The inscription at the top reads 'They feed and fight' – i.e., the peasants' labour feeds the nation, and their courage defends it. In the long run the fierceness of their attacks could not prevail against cannon and massed muskets, but their self-sacrificing courage epitomized for Poles the romantic notion of rebellion against foreign tyranny for the next 100 years and more. (Author's collection)

Heroic impression of a rebel scytheman with a Polish standard. This idealized costume came to represent the image of patriotic rebellion in Poland from 1794 through 1863. (Artist unknown; author's collection)

Crown Lands Militia Originally raised from peasants in Crown lands; those in Ukraine, Ruthenia and Wielkopolska all contributed infantry units. (The Pontoneer Battalion of the technical corps was originally formed from the Crown Militia.)

CROWN TECHNICAL CORPS

Crown Artillery Corps The corps was originally formed in 1710 by Marcin Kątski. After long stagnation it was reorganized in 1763 by Alojzy Brühl, who was named General of the Crown Artillery. In 1764 the Standing Company (*Kompanje stojące*) was formed in Warsaw; its commanders were Jozef Gembarzewski, Marjan Dyzmy Pruski and Ernest Ulrych Jaucha. In 1777 the corps was split into two brigades – Warsaw and Kamieniecz – each of three companies, each company having 393 soldiers.

Between 1764 and 1789 the black tricornes were trimmed with gold lace, white cockades and white plumes. Uniforms were green with black facings (see tables), worn with black half-boots. Officers had gold 'metal'. Long green watchcoats had yellow lace edging the cuffs and collar. In 1790 officers had a tall black *konfederatka* with a gold band and white plume. In 1793–94 NCOs had a red trouser stripe and gold NCO lace. The headgear was the infantry shako with a transverse white crest. Some sources show gunners in white trousers with boots, and a round black hat with a red plume.

Crown Engineer Corps The corps was formed by the Sejm in 1775 under the overall command of the Corps of Artillery. In 1791 they organized a company of pioneers. Between 1772 and 1789 the rank of conductor had gold lace on the collar, cuffs and lapels. Black round hats had gold lace and white cockades, and black boots were worn. Officers had gold epaulettes. In 1790–94 the corps included sappers, pictured with an infantry shako with brass plate and white plume. Officers wore a dark green *konfederatka* with a gold above a white band, white cords and white plume.

Crown Pioneer Corps The Pioneer Corps was formed from militia companies in 1764. Until 1776 the officers were appointed by the war commission, and from 1777 by the king. The pioneers were stationed in Warsaw and Praga, then in Nieszawa and Nowe Dwory. At the time of the Kosciuszko Insurrection the Pioneers were absorbed into the 16th Foot Regt.

ARMY OF THE GRAND DUCHY: LITHUANIAN CAVALRY

Horse Guards Regiment of the Grand Duchy of Lithuania The Horse Guards were formed in 1717 as a dragoon regiment, originally titled the *Lejbregiment Dragonow Krolewskich Wielkiego Ksiestwa Litewskiego*. From 1762 it was known as the *Regiment Konny Krola Imci Wielkiego Ksiestwa Litewskiego*; from 1784, as the *Regiment Gwardii Konnej Wielkiego Ksiestwa Litewskiego*; and in 1793 it became the *Regiment Karabinierow Gwardii Konnej Litewskiej*.

(S) Grodno & Pruzany (1783–92). (B) Bar civil war. In 1792 there is a note of gold epaulettes, and a black side-to-side bicorne with gold lace and white plume.

1st Lithuanian National Cavalry Brigade, a.k.a. Hussars of Kowienska (F) 1776. (S) Kowno & Minsk (1789), Kiejdany (1790), Wilkomierz, Poniewież, Rosienie, Szawle (1792). (B) Swierzen (1792), Mir; Johaniszkiele, Brzesc,

Officer of the Lithuanian Horse Guards, 1790–94. As with the footguards, these troops wore a bicorne hat side-to-side, and scarlet-red uniforms faced with blue; this officer wears gold 'metal'. Note that the coat lapels are worn buttoned across. (I. Harasimowicz, NAMW; courtesy of Arsenal.org.pl)

Poniewiez, Szczucin (1794). In 1776–85 the *towarzycz* had a red *kuczma* with black band and red plume, and a red sash. The *pocztowy* had a black *kolpak* with red plume and bag. All ranks had a white cockade.

2nd Lithuanian National Cavalry Brigade, a.k.a. Pinsk Light Horse *(F)* 1776. *(S)* Pinsk. *(B)* Mir, Dubienka (1792); at Mikolajow, Warsaw, Goluchow, Wola, Wilno, Powazki, Blonie, Maciejowice, Praga (1794).

In 1764–76, rankers of *petyhorcy* (Duchy equivalent to medium cavalry or dragoons) wore a tall felt or wool *czapka* cap stitched into a square-topped outline by vertical quilting. Officers wore the shorter *konfederatka*, and some of them still wore breastplates. In 1776–85 officers had a yellow *konfederatka* with a white cockade and plume, a blue/grey *kontusz*, and yellow boots. The *pocztowy* wore black busbies with a black plume. All ranks wore yellow trousers with a blue sidestripe and bottom band. In 1792 the *towarzycz* is depicted in a shako with the front visor upturned. The lances were spirally striped in the colours of the pennant.

3rd Lithuanian National Cavalry Brigade *(F)* 1792. *(S)* Rosienie. *(B)* Wilno (1794).

1st Advance Guard Regiment of HM the Grand Duke of Lithuania *(F)* 1776, as light *ulans*. *(S)* Onikszty, Rzeczyca (1789), Cholopienicze (1790), Widze (1792). *(B)* Opsa, Mscibow, Wojszkami (1792). Transferred into Russian army as Lithuanian-Tartar Regt.

2nd Advance Guard Regiment Grand Hetman of Lithuania Josef Jelenski *(F)* 1776, from light cavalry. *(S)* Borysow, Mozyrz (1789), Mariampol (1790), Wilkomierz, Onikszty (Oct 1792). *(B)* Praga (1794). In 1776–89 officers had silver epaulettes, and a red *konfederatka* with white cockade and plume. Troopers had no shoulder straps; *towarzyczy* had red belts.

3rd Advance Guard Regiment Field Hetman of Lithuania Antoni Chlewinkiego *(F)* 1776. *(S)* Mozyrz & Lojow (1789), Mozyrz (1790), Strzeszyn (1791),Wilkowyszki (Oct 1792). *(B)* Zelwa (1792); Krupczyce, Brzesc, Maciejowice, Praga (1794).

A plume-holder now in the National Army Museum and dating from 1776–89 is yellow metal enamelled with the king's cypher (turquoise), crown (blue and gold), wreath (blue with red ribbons) and metal feathers (turquoise and red). Troopers had blue shoulder straps on the left side; *towarzycz* had blue belts; officers, a blue *konfederatka* with white cockade and plume.

4th Lithuanian Advance Guard Regiment of Josef Bielaki *(F)* 1733, from Potocki's Tartar cavalry in Voivodeship of Kijowski. *(S)* Kamieniec Litewski (1782–87), Borysow (1790). *(B)* Bar civil war; Swierzenic, Mir (1792); Zelwa, Izabelin, Mscibow, Brzesc, Dereczyn, Maciejowice, Praga (1794). In 1776–89 the *towarzycz* had red belts and plumes, the rankers white belts. Officers had white plumes, and all had white cockades.

5th Lithuanian Advance Guard Regiment of Stanislaw Byszewski *(F)* as above; entered state service 1764. After Bar civil war, *(S)* Suchowola (1772), Krynki (1789), Wielona (Oct 1792). *(B)* 1792 War; Praga (1794). In 1764–89 officers wore green waistcoat with gold lace; officers and *towarzycz* white feathers, and all a white cockade; *towarzyczy* had a green belt/sash.

Tartar Regiment of Jacob Azulewicz, King's Militia – a.k.a. 2nd Regt Nadwornie Ulans (*2 Pulk Ulan Nadwornych***), and 6th Lithuanian Advance Guard Regt (***6 Pulk Litewski Przedniej Strazy***).** *(S)* Kobryn & Lomna (Dec 1792). *(B)* Wilno (1794).

Uniforms of front and second-rank troopers of the 2nd Lithuanian Advance Guard Regt between 1780 and 1789. After the First Partition the light cavalry were reorganized into Advance Guard regiments, building on the uniform traditions of the previous half-century. (General Research Division, NYC Public Library, Astor, Lenox and Tilden Foundations)

Azulewicz's militia regiment of Tartars in the service of the Grand Duchy, 1780s. In 1792 this was known as the 2nd King's Lancers, and later as the 6th Lithuanian Advance Guard Regiment. The uniform illustrated is a yellow cap, and a red *katanka* trimmed with yellow, over a yellow *zupan* with red cuffs, yellow trousers and yellow boots. The lance and pennant are red and yellow. (I. Harasimowicz, NAMW; courtesy of Arsenal.org.pl)

LEFT
Musketeer, Lithuanian Foot Guard Regt, 1790–94. The hat lace is gold, the pompon white-over-red. The red coat is faced and lined dark blue, with yellow-metal buttons. The tight Hungarian breeches are dark blue, with gold knots embroidered on the thighs. (I. Harasimowicz, NAMW; courtesy of Arsenal.org.pl)

RIGHT
Grenadier, Lithuanian Foot Guard Regt, 1790–94. Guard troops are the only units that we can confirm still had a grenadier component after 1789. In this regiment they wore a dark bearskin bonnet with a red rear patch, brass plates and white cords. At this date Crown Guard grenadiers appear to have been wearing mitre caps in summer, and bearskins with full dress. (I. Harasimowicz, NAMW; courtesy of Arsenal.org.pl)

40

Tartar Regiment of Alexander Ulano – a.k.a. 7th Regiment of Tartars of the Grand Duchy of Lithuania (7 Pulk Tartarski Wielkiego Ksiestwa Litewskiego). *(F)* May 1792. *(S)* Janow. Pressed into service of Targowica Confederation (Oct 1792). Red *czapka* with black lambswool band and white plume, and single left-hand white epaulette. The saddle cloth was red with white edging.

8th Cavalry Regiment of the Gand Duchy of Lithuania *(F)* 1794, by Gen Karwowski. *(S)* Wizma (by Oct 1794). *(B)* Magnuszew (1794).

LITHUANIAN DRAGOONS
King's Regiment of Dragoons of HM the Grand Duke of Lithuania
(F) as cavalry regt early 18th C; 1775, converted into 5th Foot Regt (qv). *(S)* Pinsk.
Horse Regiment of the Grand Hetman of the Grand Duchy of Lithuania
(F) early 18th C; 1775, converted into 2nd Foot Regt (qv).
Horse Regiment of the Field Hetman of the Grand Duchy of Lithuania
(F) early 18th C; 1775, converted into 4th Foot Regt (qv).

LITHUANIAN INFANTRY
Foot Guard Regiment of the Grand Duchy of Lithuania The regiment was stationed in Wilno (Vilnius). Its single battalion had eight companies, one of them grenadiers.

In 1770–89 grenadiers are shown both with brown bearskins with brass front plates and red plumes, and (probably in summer) brass-fronted mitre caps with white plumes. In 1790–94, grenadier bearskins had white cords; tight blue Hungarian-style breeches had gold lace thigh-knots. Musketeers and officers wore a black side-to-side bicorne with gold lace trim, the officers with black plumes. The regiment was absorbed into the Russian army on 15 April 1794.

1st Foot Regiment of the Grand Hetman of Lithuania *(F)* 1717, as the Foot Regt of the Grand Hetman of the Grand Duchy of Lithuania; 1766, designated 1st Regt of Grenadiers, and then as title above. *(S)* Borysow (1777), Slonim (1787–93), Wilkomierz (Dec 1793). *(B)* 1792 War.

In 1775–89 the black hat was trimmed with white lace and pompons, gold distinctions and button. An officer of the rifle element, 1792, is shown with a red collar, shoulder strap, lapels, turnbacks and trouser stripe, a black shako with a gold band and white cords and plume, and white belts. Enlisted men wore black leather belts.

2nd Foot Regiment of the Grand Hetman of Lithuania *(F)* 1775, from Horse Regt of the Grand Hetman (qv). *(S)* Grodno, Sokolka (1792). *(B)* Bar civil war. In 1775–89 the grenadier company had a white metal mitre-plate. In 1790–92 the jacket had pointed cuffs. Officers wore a blue *konfederatka* with white band and plume.

3rd Foot Regiment of the Field Hetman of Lithuania *(S)* Minsk (1775), Janiszki (1778), Nowogrodek/Szereszow (1778–89), Kowno (1789), Wilno (1790), Kowno (1791), Preny (Dec 1792), Szaty (1794). *(B)* 1792 War.

4th Foot Regiment of the Field Hetman of Lithuania *(F)* 1775, from Horse Regt of the Field Hetman (qv). *(S)* Brzesc, Terespol (1783), Wilno (1787–89), Borysow (1790), Minsk (1791), Sluck (1792), Zyzmory (1794). *(B)* 1792 War.

5th Lithuanian Foot Regiment of Paul George Grabowski *(F)* 30 April 1775, from King's Regt of Dragoons (qv). *(S)* Pinsk, Wilno (1778), Mscibow (1799), Wilno (1783), Brzesc (1789). *(B)* 1792 War. In 1790–92 the jacket turnbacks were dark blue with light blue edging, and the trousers had a light blue sidestripe.

6th Lithuanian Foot Regiment of Xawery Niesiolowski *(F)* 9 Dec 1775, from several independent companies. *(S)* Wilno & Nowogrodek (1790), Poniewiez (1792). *(B)* 1792 War. A picture of a grenadier,1775–89, shows a mitre cap with a brass plate backed with red. A 1783 image shows the jacket closed, with no lapels. In 1792 officers had a yellow trouser stripe, and a *konfederatka* with yellow band and white edges, cords and plume. The jacket turnbacks were dark blue with yellow edging, and the belts black.

7th Lithuanian Foot Regiment of Prince Kazimierz Nestor Sapiehia *(F)* from several independent companies, during the Great Sejm; a.k.a. *fizyliers*. *(S)* Oszmianka & Wilno (1791), Smorgonie (1791), Oszmiana (1792), Wilno & Smorgonie (1794). *(B)* 1792 War.

8th Lithuanian Foot Regiment of the House of Radziwiłł *(F)* 1 March 1790, from several independent companies. *(S)* Nieswiez & Czarnobyl (1791), Nieswiez (1792), Plonsk & Stwolowicze (1793). *(B)* 1792 War. In 1790–94 they had round cuffs. The officer's *konfederatka* was dark blue with white piping, band, cords and plume.

9th Lithuanian Foot Regiment *(F)* 1794, during Kosciuszko Insurrection.

Independent units:

Grand Hetman of Lithuania's Hungarian Rifle Company *(F)* 1717, retained until 1793. Uniformed like the Crown Hungarian companies, but with yellow facings.

Field Hetman of Lithuania's Hungarian Company *(F)* 1717, retained until 1793. Considered as the Grenadiers of the Grand Duchy's army.

Officer, Lithuanian Corps of Riflemen, 1790–94. This depiction of an officer of the Grand Duchy's consolidated corps of four rifle battalions shows the uniform as green with red facings and a gold epaulette, worn with black 'Hessian' boots. Interestingly, he wears a flat-topped round hat instead of the domed Lithuanian *Raupenhelm*; it has a brass bottom band, and a white plume and cords. (I. Harasimowicz, NAMW; courtesy of Arsenal.org.pl)

Hungarian Company of the Lithuanian Court of Justice *(S)* Mejszagola & Szyrwinty (1792).

Grand Marshal of Lithuania's Hungarian Company *(F)* 1717, retained until 1794.

Grand Hetman of Lithuania's Janissary Company This company wore uniforms similar to those of the Grand Hetman of the Crown's Janissaries, but with a red hat, and a red jacket over a white kaftan, both edged with black.

Field Hetman of Lithuania's Janissary Company

MISCELLANEOUS DUCHY TROOPS

Crown Lands Militia In 1763 there was a company of Grenadiers from the Crown Lands. In 1777 there was a Militia Corps of the Crown, and a battalion of pontoneers. In 1789 a battalion was raised from the Crown Lands, and in 1794 this and the Pontoneer Corps were absorbed into the the Crown 16th Foot Regiment. The commanders were Capt Skwarczynski (1763), Col Markowski (1777), Col de Woyten (1788) and Col Jan Gisiler (1794). *(B)* Warsaw (1794).

Grand Duchy of Lithuania Lands Militia (*Milicja Skarbu W. Ks. Litewskiego*) *(S)* Grodno. Commanders were *Rotmister* Wojnillowicz, Tadeusz Suchodolec (1783) and Jan Karbowski (1793).

2nd Grodno Battalion of the King and Commonwealth In 1790 this unit was absorbed into 7th Lithuanian Foot Regt (qv). Commanders were Maj Jan Müntz (1783) and Capt Jan Möser (1785–91).

Garrison of Czestochowa Commander was Maj Marcin Wierzbowski (1787).

LITHUANIAN TECHNICAL CORPS

Lithuanian Corps of Artillery (*Korpus Artylerii Litewskiej*) The commanders of the Corps were Gens Branicki (1768) and Kazimierz Nestor Saphieha (1773). The Company of Cannoneers was stationed in Wilno (1773); its commanders were Capts Montresor (1773), Marcin Wolk (1774) and Vietynghoff (1779 – promoted major in 1787).

In 1775–89 the black tricornes had gold lace trim and white cockades; the gunners wore brass-fronted mitres with red plate-backing, and green coats with black cuffs, lapels and turnbacks, over white waistcoats. In 1792 the artillery had *kurtka* uniforms in the same colours, and gold epaulettes; the black *Raupenhelm* had a brass band and black plume. Some officers wore a dark green *litewka* with black collar and cuffs; their *konfederatka* had a dark green top, and a white band above a black lambswool band. Trousers were dark green with a black sidestripe. Generals of artillery are pictured in a high-crowned hat with a gold band, and the left brim turned up and fixed with a white cockade and plume. The plumes and lace are sometimes depicted as red.

The Free Company of Grenadiers was stationed in Wilno (1773), commanded by Capt Freyderyk Wilhielm Cronenmann (1773, promoted lieutenant-colonel 1781) and Captain Antoni Godin (1781). In 1770–89 the grenadiers wore brass-fronted mitres with red plate-backing, and green coats and waistcoats with red lapels, cuffs and turnbacks.

Lithuanian Engineer Corps Only formed in the late 18th century, this took part in the 1794 Kosciuszko Insurrection. Under its Chief (General of Artillery Sapieha) it was commanded by Jakob Jasinski.

Bombadier of Lithuanian Artillery, 1790–94. The green uniform has a black collar, cuffs, sidestripe, and piping around green lapels and turnbacks. The *Raupenhelm* has a black top crest and side plume, and a brass band. (I. Harasimowicz 1792, NAMW, courtesy of Arsenel.org.pl)

ARMY OF THE TARGOWICA CONFEDERATION, 1792–93

National Cavalry Brigade of Hussars of the Commander of Kiev *(F)* June 1792. *(S)* Krasne & Czerkasy. Transferred into Russian army (June 1793) as Bohski Regt.
Wore a crimson cap and distinctions, with a blue *kurtka* and trousers.

National Cavalry Brigade 'Golden Liberty' of the Commander of Podlaski Date and uniform as above.

National Cavalry Brigade of Hussars of the Commander of Braclaw Date and uniform as above; *(S)* Granow.

Light Cavalry Regiment of Human *(F)* June 1792. *(S)* Tulczyn & Brzostowica (March 1793) Transferred into Russian army (June 1793) as Winnicki Regt.

Kiev Light Cavalry Regiment See 1st & 3rd Loyal Cossacks, under 'Crown Cavalry'.

Advance Guard Regiment of the Free Confederation Transferred into Russian army (June 1793) as Owrucki Regt.

Infantry Regiment of the Free Confederation Taken into service of Confederation with 15 companies; *(S)* Tulczyn. Troops depicted in a blue-over-white *konfederatka* with a black band and white plume, and dark blue *kurtka* and trousers.

The patriotic cult of Kosciuszko is exemplified by this magnificent 1794 gilded sword belt plate bearing an enamelled portrait of him set against trophies of arms and flags. (NAMW; author's collection)

SELECT BIBLIOGRAPHY

Anusiewicz, Marion (ed) & Bronislaw Gembarzeski, *Zolnierz polsk od 1697 do 1794 roku* (Wydawnictwo Ministerstwa Obrony Narodowej; Warsaw, 1963)

www.Arsenal.org.pl., *Rekonstrukcja mundura towarzysza Kawalerii Narodowej Koronnej z lat 1791–1794* (2011)

www.Arsenal.org.pl., *Brygada i Kawalerii narodowej* (2009)

Cranz, Philip, *The Army of the Grand Duchy of Warsaw: Vol III Infantry* (Uniformology; Weatherford, 2008)

Czop, Jan, *Barwa Wojska Rzeczypospolitej Obojga narodów w XVIII wieku* (Libra; Rzeszow, 2009)

Davies, Norman, *God's Playground: History of Poland, Vols I, II* (Columbia University Press; New York, 1982)

Gembarzeski, Bronislaw, *Rodowody Pułkow Polskich i Oddziałow Rownorzednych od r 1717 do r 1831. Nakladem* (Tow Wiedzy Wojskowej; Warsaw, 1925)

Haiman, Miecislaus, *Kosciuszko: Leader and Exile* (Kosciuszko Foundation; New York, 1977)

Jedruch, Jacek, *Constitutions, Elections and Legislatures of Poland, 1493–1993: A Guide to their History* (EJJ Books; New York, 1998)

Kannik, Preben, *Military Uniforms of the World in Color* (Macmillan Publishing Co, Inc; New York, 1974)

Kaplan, Herbert H., *The First Partition of Poland* (Columbia University Press; New York,1962)

Knotel, Richard, Herbert Knotel & Herbert Sieg, *Uniforms of the World* (Charles Scribner & Son; New York, 1980)

Kom, Eduk. Narod, *Regulamen Exercerunku dla Regimentow Konnych Gwardyi* (Drukarni Nadworney; Warsaw, 1786)

Korbal, Rafat, *Dzieje Wojska Polskiego* (Wydawnictwo Podsiedlik-Raniowski I Spolka; Poznan, 1990)

Lubicz-Pachonski, Jan, *Bitwa pod Raclawicami* (Panstwowe Wydawnictwo Naukowe; Warsaw, 1984)

Maslowski, Maciej, *Juliusz Kossak* (Wydawnictwa Artystyczne i Filmowe; Warsaw, 1982)

www.muzeumwp.pl

Pachonski, Jan, *General Jan Henryk Dabrowski 1755–1818* (Wydawnictwo Ministerstwa Obrony Narodowej; Warsaw, 1981)

Pachonski, Jan, *Legiony Polskie: Prawda i Legenda 1794–1807* (Wydawnictwo Ministerstwa Obrony Narodowej; Warsaw, 1979)

Pogonowski, Iwo Cyprian, *Poland: A Historical Atlas* (Hippocrene Books, Inc; New York, 1987)

Ratajczyk, Leonard & Jerzy Teodorczyk, *Wojsko Powstania Kosciuszkowskiego* (Wydawnictwo Ministerstwa Obrony Narodowej; Warsaw, 1987)

Ratajczyk, Leonard, *Wojsko i obronnosc Rzeczypospolitej 1788 – 1792* (Wydawnictwo Ministerstwa Obrony Narodowej; Warsaw, 1975)

Skowronek, Jerzy, *Ksiaze Jozef Poniatowski* (Ossonlineum; Wroclaw, 1984)

Smolinski, Aleksander, *Munur I Barwy artylerii polskiej w XVIII I XIX wieku* (Wydawnictwo Naukowe Uniwersytetu Milkołaja Koperniki; Torun, 2010)

Storozynski, Alex, *The Peasant Prince* (St Martins Press; New York, 2009)

Twardowski, Boleslaw, *Wojsko Polskie Kosciuszki w roku 1794* (Nakladem Ksiegarni Katolickiej; Poznan, 1894)

Zamoyski, Adam, *Poland: A History* (Harper Press; London, 2009)

Zamoyski, Adam, *The Last King of Poland* (Cape; London, 1992)

Zygulski, Zdzislaw & Henryk Wielecki, *Polski mundur wojskowy* (Krajowa Agencja Wydawnicza w Krakowie; Krakow, 1988)

PLATE COMMENTARIES

A: THE BAR CONFEDERATION, 1768–70

The Bar Confederates were originally clothed in a mixture of Polish military and civilian garb. By 1770 they had managed to capture several cities, including Krakow, and several magnates ruled the Confederation as an independent state until the fall of Jasna Gora in August 1772 effectively ended the uprising.

A1: Cavalryman, 1768

Cavalry of the Confederation looked similar in style to the government cavalry. The uniform of this minor nobleman is based on items in the National Army Museum, particularly a white jacket in the *kurtka* style, faced with crimson. It is worn here with a red *konfederatka* cap and trousers. Many troopers wore large gorgets – often depicting the Black Madonna, or a Maltese cross – as a nod to their armoured heritage.

A2: Officer, Wielkopolska, 1770

Confederate officers were often recognized leaders of a clan or group that could be amalgamated with others into larger formations to take the field against Russian and royal troops. This officer from Great Poland wears an approximation of the uniform of *pancerni* medium cavalry: a dark blue jacket faced red, worn over a long red *zupan*, with silver buttons. Because so many Barists wore the square hat, it became synonymous with the Confederation – thus '*konfederatka*'. The particular

height and shape of the *konfederatka* in fact varied widely, and this 'onion' form was fashionable.Yellow shoes or boots dated from the 17th century as a sign of wealth or nobility.

A3: Infantryman, 1770

Initially the peasant followers and retainers of the leaders would be clothed by their masters, in some cases with a belted linen over-shirt and a long-sleeved coat belted around the waist (see Plate G). As time went on uniforms and equipment were supplied at first by Prussia and later by Austria, leading to them acquiring the semblance of a uniformed army. This example is based on a description, in the diary of a participant, of the 'Western'-style infantry uniforms in use from c.1770. He is holding a banner of Karol Radziwill, one of the leaders of the Confederation; obscured here, the inscription 'MONSTRATE/ESSE MATREM' flanks an image of the Virgin, between wreathed Polish eagles and 'KR' cyphers in the corners, and trophies of arms centred on the edges.

B: CAVALRY, 1770s

This decade saw several transitions in organization and uniforms, and these cavalrymen reflect the older styles that were probably still seen for some time after the reforms ordered in 1774.

B1: *Towarzycz* of Crown Hussars, c.1770

Line cavalry units retained the old distinction between two categories of soldiers in the ranks, the superior *towarzycz* 'comrade' and the ordinary *pocztowy* trooper, the former typically riding in the front rank with a lance. The officer's tall quilted cap, reminiscent of an old Tartar style, had a blue top with white edging over a black band, and white feathers, while that of the 'comrades' had a red top. Officers wore the red *kontusz* – an over-jacket with split sleeves – lined in white, with dark blue facings, over a white *zupan*; the 'comrades' had a medium blue *zupan* and facings. This lance pennant is halved in the uniform colours, red over blue. Waist sashes at this period were usually fastened by being 'wrapped around themselves' on the left side. The saddle cloth was red with blue edging. This figure is based on a painting by Canaletto in Anusiewicz.

B2: *Pocztowy* of National Cavalry, Wielkopolska, 1776
In 1776 the cavalry was organized into national brigades, at first grouped by region and numbered (e.g. 1st Wielkopolski), and later simply numbered. The 'retainers' or troopers typically wore a plainer version of National Cavalry uniform in reversed colours from that of the 'comrades', with a headgear that varied according to the unit's home region – here, like the officers, a *konfederatka*. The medium blue jacket faced with red is worn over a white waistcoat edged with blue. Note the scalloped blue sidestripe and bottom edging on the red trousers (riding overalls), and the leather reinforcements. Troopers were typically armed with a sword, carbine and pistol; this man might have an Austrian carbine, which was hooked and strapped to its sling belt in a butt-down position.

B3: *Towarzycz*, 2nd Advance Guard Regiment (Jelenski's), Grand Duchy of Lithuania, late 1770s
The advance guards were organized as light cavalry regiments. They were uniformed in an 'oriental' style of dress, with a decorative short-sleeved *katanka* jacket worn over a long-sleeved *kontusz* or *zupan*, usually with the garments and their facings in contrasting colours. Here the *katanka* is light blue with orange-ochre facings, the *zupan* orange-ochre with light blue pointed single-button cuffs, the trousers orange-ochre with light blue sidestripes and bottom edging, and the cap crown matching the *zupan*. In the Grand Duchy the lances were striped spirally in the same colours as the lance pennant, usually reflecting the basic and facing colours of the uniform. The sword is of the *karabela* type.

C: INFANTRY, 1770s
Line infantry of the 1770s were dressed in keeping with the styles they inherited in part from the Saxon monarchy, and in part from traditional Commonwealth troop types.

C1: Janissary Company of the Grand Hetman of the Crown, 1770
Janissaries served as elite bodyguards of key military leaders, and were uniformed in the tradition of their Ottoman namesakes. Officers wore a red fez with a white turban and white plume. Their over-jacket was a red *katanka* with gold lace and epaulettes and black edging, worn over a white *zupan* edged black and trimmed with gold lace, and red trousers. By the 1790s these units had been phased out in the Crown armies, but they were retained in the Duchy's organization until the end of the Commonwealth.

C2: Grenadier NCO, Lithuanian Footguard Regiment (Czartoryski's), 1775
The Crown and Duchy footguard regiments were both modelled on the Saxon Guards, thus the red uniform coat in contrast to the blue worn by the Duchy's Line units. These units were the single constant in the armed forces during the troubled early period of King Stanislaw August's reign, and reported directly to him. This sergeant wears a grenadier's mitre cap with a brass plate and a red-and-white ostrich-feather plume attached centrally at the back, and a grenadier's belly-box with extra cartridges in addition to the pouch on his crossbelt. His coat has a small falling collar; the buttons are yellow metal – 7 on the lapels, 3 below the right lapel, 3 on the pockets and 2 on the cuffs. His rank is indicated by gold lace on his lapels and cuffs, and by his cane.

C3: Musketeer, 1st Foot Regiment of the Crown 'Queen Jadwiga' (Golcz's), 1779
The Line regiments of the Crown and Duchy were uniformed like most contemporary European infantry, in a tricorne hat; a long-tailed coat with a small collar and open lapels, facing-coloured collar, lapels and cuffs, and white lining at the tail turnbacks; a waistcoat, knee-breeches, and long black cloth marching gaiters. The Crown regiments wore red coats, the Duchy's blue, but otherwise they were very similar. The hat is trimmed with white tape and has corner pompons in black (this regiment's facing colour) over white. The coat has white metal buttons; the neck stock is red; and the smallclothes and the leather equipment are all white, the latter with brass buckles. The shoulder belt supports a large cartridge pouch, and the waist belt a brass-hilted 'hanger' sword; as usual, the scabbard is covered in black leather with brass fittings.

D: CROWN GUARDS, 1790s
The Guard was the backbone of the army, and was involved in most major campaigns from the suppression of the Bar Confederation, through the War in Defence of the Constitution, to the siege of Warsaw during the Kosciuszko Insurrection.

D1: Musketeer, Crown Foot Guard Regiment (Poniatowski's), 1792
The extensive army reforms of 1788–89 saw the introduction for the infantry and artillery of the classic *kurtka* jacket, with regimental facing colours on the standing collar, shoulder straps, lapels, cuffs, rear seams and frontal turnbacks. The culminating ordinance of March 1791, of which the provisions were in place on the eve of the war with Russia in 1792, included the introduction of a shako for Crown troops. The Crown footguard regiment differed from the Duchy unit (Jablonowski's) in wearing this 1791 *casquet*, while the Lithuanian unit continued to wear bicorne hats and grenadier bearskins. The brass plate on the separate frontal flap bears a Polish eagle, and has a milled white-metal edging. Note the dark moose- or horsehair crest or roach, formed around a wire armature and fixed centrally from bottom rear to top front, and the white-over-black plume fixed vertically on the left. The Guard regiment continued to wear red, here the 1788–89 *kurtka* faced in medium blue; in addition to those fixing the two shoulder straps there are 8 paired buttons on each lapel and 2 on each cuff. The trousers are medium blue with a 2cm yellow sidestripe, and hang free over the half-boots, with 'stirrup' straps. The hanger has a brass hilt and scabbard-fittings; the brass belt plate bears a Polish eagle device. Stachowitz shows Line infantry wearing small Prussian cowhide knapsacks slung behind the left hip over the hanger, and a cartridge box plate with what might be either a Prussian or a Polish eagle; we therefore choose to give this Guard figure a Prussian 1782 musket. One later reconstruction also shows a man of the Crown footguards wearing Hungarian-style uniform, with pointed jacket cuffs, and tight breeches decorated with 'knots' on the thighs, worn tucked into half-boots.

D2: Dragoon, Crown Guard Dragoons (Potocki's), 1792

In addition to the crimson *kurtka* with light blue facings, the Guard Dragoons adopted what we today call a 'Tarleton'-style leather helmet, of the light dragoon type seen widely in the last quarter of the century. One example in the Polish National Army Museum has a brass horizontal band with a protruding rim, a leather visor and raised 'comb', and a horsehair crest or mane; another has this large plate, but no sign of a mane on the comb. A portrait of Prince Jozef Poniatowski in the uniform of the Guard Dragoons shows a leopardskin turban wrapped around the base. The Lithuanian Horse Guards (Stryjenski's) seem to have retained their dragoon-style bicorne, but otherwise adopted this uniform. We have chosen to give this dragoon a Prussian rifled carbine.

D3: Gunner, Crown Guard Horse Artillery, 1794

At the time of the Kosciuszko Insurrection the Crown Guard Horse Artillery were distinguished by a round black visored 'jockey-cap' headgear with a brass band. Their green *kurtka* and trousers had red facings and sidestripes and yellow-metal buttons, and their leather belting was white.

E: LINE INFANTRY, 1790s
E1: Musketeer, 2nd Crown Foot Regiment 'Crown Prince' (Wodzicki's)

The *kurtka* was authorized for all units by 1789; the two shoulder straps were either piped (as here) or made wholly in the regimental facing colour – for this unit, crimson. Trousers were of white linen in the summer, and of dark blue wool with a facing-colour sidestripe for wintertime. The personal equipment and some of the muskets were apparently of Prussian manufacture or modelled on Prussian patterns; while older Polish weapons certainly continued in use, we have chosen to show him with a Prussian musket. Two battalions of this regiment fought under Kosciuszko at Raclawice in April 1794.

E2: Musketeer, 5th Lithuanian Foot Regiment (Grabowski's)

In place of the 1791 shako, the Line regiments of the Grand Duchy received a taller felt headgear with a domed top; this resembled the leather *'Raupenhelm'* adopted by Bavarian troops a few years later. It had the same type of crest or roach as the Crown shako attached from the base of the back to the top, and a conventional white plume on the left. One surviving example in the Polish National Army Museum has deep fold-up flaps on the back and sides, the words *Rex et Patria* ('King and Fatherland') cut out of the brass band, and a

stamped pewter badge of the Polish eagle above this. It is possible that some bore the Lithuanian 'armoured horseman' badge instead **(see inset)**. Paul George Grabowski's 5th Lithuanian Foot Regt wore sky-blue facings; note – just visible under the haversack and sword – the turnback style adopted by some regiments, of uniform blue edged with facing colour trim rather than of solid facing colour.

E3: Rifleman, 10th Crown Foot Regiment (Dzialynski's)

By 1789 a small platoon of sharpshooters with rifles were a component of Commonwealth battalions; in 1791 they were gathered in a company per regiment; in 1792 the Grand Duchy formed a four-battalion Rifle Corps, and in April 1794 Crown riflemen formed at least one full regiment (19th Foot, Sokolnicki's). They wore round hats with flat tops, often with the brim turned up on the left side. Most wore green uniforms of the universal *kurtka* style, with the facings of their parent regiments. This veteran, his uniform faded by the sun and rain, is lucky to have received a German Jaeger-style rifle. The leather equipment was sometimes blackened.

F: NATIONAL CAVALRY, 1790s

The cavalry reforms of 1789–91 created a standard uniform. The *rogatywka* lancer cap was about 17cm (6.7in) in height and 17.5cm (7in) square at the top, though not yet rigidly stiffened. The *kurtka* had a 7cm (2.75in) standing collar, lapels measuring 5.5cm wide and 49cm long (2.1in x 19.3in), and cuffs 9.5cm deep (3.7in), all in the facing colour. The jacket was secured by hooks-and-eyes, with seven buttons on each side; the turnbacks were sewn down, but there was a button on the left shoulder for an epaulette. The back seams of the body and sleeves were trimmed with 0.5cm (0.2in) facing-colour piping, as were three-pointed, three-buttoned diagonal pocket flaps. The trousers were reinforced in the crotch and/or inside legs; they closed at the ankle with buttons, and a 'stirrup' strap looped under the instep.

F1: Officer, 1st National Cavalry Brigade

This uniform is taken from surviving items and a number of contemporary coloured depictions. It is in the *towarzycz* style, with a lancer cap bearing a badge with the king's cypher on the white cockade, offset to the left front at the base of a white feather plume. The dark blue *kurtka* faced with crimson bears two silver epaulettes of rank, and the crimson trousers have two white sidestripes. The pouch belt, echoing the silver and crimson of the waist sash, supports a pouch with a gilt cover behind the back. Badges of rank on the epaulettes were of a different sequence to that used in the Advance Guard regiments, dragoons, infantry and artillery; the two diagonal bars identify a lieutenant in the National Cavalry.

F2: *Pocztowy*, 1st National Cavalry Brigade

Also from contemporary depictions, this trooper's uniform is basically similar, but with a mirliton or *giwer* cap trimmed with white cords rather than a *rogatywka*; the cap badge is similar, but the plume is white-over-black. The *kurtka* has one white woolen epaulette on the left. Belt equipment is whitened, and the sabre has a white woollen wrist strap.

Flamboyant impressions of the parade uniforms of a *rotmistrz* and a *towarzycz* of the 1st Wielkopolski National Cavalry Bde in 1790; compare with Plate F1. The reforms of the Great Sejm (1788-92) sought to transform the army from a 'regional' to a 'national' organization, with the beginings of standardized uniform. (Originals in NAMW, artist unknown; author's collection)

F3: *Towarzycz*, 2nd Advance Guard Regiment of the Crown, 1792

Advance Guard units functioned as light cavalry, and wore a blue or green *kurtka* depending on the unit. The elite trooper's *rogatywka* is crimson with a black band, and a white plume above the badge. This regiment wore medium green jackets with black facings and distinctions, and crimson trousers with double black sidestripes. The *towarzycz's* lance was painted in spiral black and green stripes, with a green-over-black pennant. His equipment is otherwise the same as that of F2.

G: PEASANT MILITIA; RACLAWICE, 1794

When Koscuszko proclaimed the Insurrection, troops that had been designated for demobilization, and in some cases those transferred to Russian service, rallied to his banner, and all able-bodied men between 18 and 40 years of age were mobilized – even if they could only be armed with scythes. On 7 May 1794, Kosciuszko issued the Polaniec Proclamation freeing the serfs. He believed that serfdom was wrong in itself, and, based on his experience in the American Revolution, he believed that men would be motivated to fight if they had genuine liberties to defend. (Kosciuszko's education and international experience had moved him politically well to the 'left' of most Polish noblemen, but the obviously disastrous consequences of the 1792 Targowica Confederation widened his appeal even among reactionaries.) Unfortunately, this liberal measure only had force in regions where Kosciuszko could exercise personal command; but in April 1794 some 2,000 of these lightly-armed peasants played a major role in defeating a Russian corps near Krakow.

G1: Scytheman, Krakow 'Grenadiers'

The peasant militia from the Krakow region were given the title of 'Grenadiers' after proving their worth at Raclawice, and thereafter they were employed as shock troops. The primary source for these uniforms is Michal Stachowicz's drawing of 'the Polish Army in Camps in 1794', but there are other period depictions and items in museums. One drawing clearly shows the peacock-feather plume on this volunteer's *konfederatka*. The typical off-white *sukmana* overcoat, with red cuffs and red lining is decorated at collar and breast with lines of black and red embroidery. Note the very broad leather belly-band (*trzos*), and the grey blanket-roll. The commander of the 1st Regt of Grenadiers was depicted wearing a black felt round hat with a green plume, and a white *sukmana* with a red collar and cuffs and black decorative embroidery, over dark blue trousers with a crimson stripe. The epaulette on his right shoulder and the lace on his collar were silver; around his waist he wore a red sash, and his shoulder belt was black with a gilt plate.

G2: Musketeer, Sandomierz 'Grenadiers'

Only about 300 of the 2,000 peasant fighters at Raclawice had muskets. This one, from the Sandomierz region, sports a sprig of green leaves on his woollen cap; his *sukmana* is russet brown with red and white trim and cord details. These coats were worn over a white belted shirt-tunic, and wool trousers tucked into sturdy boots. His traditional 'chiming' belt has decorative loops of strap strung with pierced brass discs, and contemporary drawings show hatchets carried as close-quarter weapons.

Peasant scythemen, pikemen, musketeers and cavalry during the Kosciuszko Insurrection, drawn by Stachowicz in 1804 – see Plate G. They wear a motley collection of headgear and personal clothing, and broad-brimmed round hats are by no means particular to the horsemen. However, their general use of overcoats gave them a kind of uniformity of appearance. (Michal Stachowicz, NAMW; author's collection)

G3: Militia cavalryman

During the Insurrection those better-off peasant farmers who were accustomed to riding and who acquired horses were grouped into auxiliary cavalry units, to fulfill the same scouting and skirmishing roles as Cossacks. They are depicted (e.g. by Stachowicz, and later Knötel) with broad-brimmed black hats with a green plume on the left; white coats trimmed with black, apparently cut shorter than the *sukmana*; blue trousers with a red sidestripe; black leather belts; swords and muskets; and lances with white-over-green or white-over-black pennants. Saddle cloths seem to have been white with black edging, or blue with red edging.

H: WARSAW, 1794

H1: Tadeusz Kosciuszko

Poland's most famous national hero was portrayed in many paintings; this image is based on portraits by Kossack and Stachowitz, and on his surviving coat and other items in the National Army Museum, Warsaw. Despite his rank of lieutenant-general Kosciuszko habitually wore over his uniform *kurtka* and sash a *sukmana* overcoat typical of the peasants in the Krakow region. The coat has deteriorated, but a later reconstruction with gold cord trim in place of what seems to be the orginal black seems less convincing. Kosciuszko was among the first to receive Poland's highest decoration, the *Virtuti Militari* cross, for his service in the 1792 campaign.

H2: Engineer officer, Grand Duchy

By the 1790s the professional quality of the Commonwealth's young officer corps was high. The artillery, engineers and pontoneers wore uniforms of the same design as the infantry, but in a medium green colour faced and lined with black. This ensign has an officer's *konfederatka* in a slightly darker shade, with a black band trimmed with gold lace, a white cockade and plume. The rear edge of the black turnbacks on his *kurtka* also display a line of gold lace, and he wears two gold epaulettes of rank. The black trousers have a medium green sidestripe. The officers' epaulette badges of rank in most branches were one, two and three stars for ensign to captain; a narrow diagonal stripe for major, and one, two and three wide diagonals for lieutenant colonel, colonel and colonel-in-chief.

H3: NCO, Crown Artillery

This artillery sergeant is also uniformed in green faced with black, but his trousers are green with a gold stripe. His other distinctions of rank are double gold lace stripes on his collar and cuffs. The most

immediately obvious difference from the infantry uniform is the white crest or roach arranged from side to side over the top of his shako, which also has a white left-side plume. (Some infantrymen are also pictured with white transverse crests; it has been suggested that these represent grenadiers within the regiments, which seem to have been discontinued in 1791–94.) The NCO's cap device shows crossed cannons below a flaming shell; his sidearm is a standard brass-hilted infantry hanger.

INDEX